Discover the Art of Crafting Exquisite Tarts and Ta...

100 Mouthwatering Recipes for Every Occasion

Pamela Morris

Copyright Material

©2023 GILBERT C.A

All Rights Reserved

No part of this book may be used or transmitted in any form or by any means without the proper written consent of the publisher and copyright owner, except for brief quotations used in a review. This book should not be considered a substitute for medical, legal, or other professional advice.

TABLE OF CONTENTS

TABLE OF CONTENTS..3
INTRODUCTION...8
CRUST AND SHELLS..9
1. Basic Flaky Pie Crust...10
2. The Unshrinkable Sweet Tart Shell..12
3. Cheese tart shells..15
4. Cornmeal crust tart shell...17
5. Free-form tart shells...19
6. Chocolate crust...21
7. Graham crust..23
8. Mini Tart Shells..25
9. French Sweet Tart Crust...28
10. Cream Cheese Tart Shells...30
11. Walnut Tartlet Shells..32
12. Phyllo Tart Shells..34
13. Shortbread Tart Crust...36
14. Eggless Tart Crust...39
15. Whole Wheat Tart Crust...42
CHOCOLATE TARTS..44
16. Truffle tart with espresso sauce..45
17. Dark Chocolate Tart with Gingersnap Crust.....................48
18. Chocolate brownie tart...51
19. Chocolate butter tarts...54
20. Chocolate coconut mini tarts...56

21. Chocolate hazelnut tart..58
22. Chocolate mascarpone nut tart.......................................61
23. Chocolate miniature tarts..64
24. Chocolate truffle tart with raspberries.........................66
25. Cranberry and white chocolate tart..............................69
26. Double chocolate cream tart...72
27. Fudgy chocolate tart...75
28. Fresh fruit and chocolate tart......................................77
29. Spicy chocolate tart..80
30. Strawberry white chocolate mousse tart.....................82
31. Swedish chocolate dessert konungens tarts................85
32. White chocolate banana crème tart.............................88
33. Wicked dark chocolate tart..91
SEAFOOD TARTS...94
34. Alaska seafood tarts...95
35. Crawfish and spicy cheese tart....................................97
36. Scallops and blue cheese tart......................................99
37. Creamy smoked salmon and dill tart.........................101
38. Norwegian salmon tarts...104
39. Tiny smoked salmon tarts...107
40. Festive shrimp tarts...109
41. Shrimp, onion, and tomato tart.................................111
42. Shrimp cocktail tarts...114
NUT TARTS..116
43. Almond tart..117
44. Mexican Chocolate Tart with Spiced Pecans.............120
45. Frangipane Tart with seasonal Fruit.........................123

46. Bakewell Tart..126
47. Apple nut lattice tart..128
48. Apricot macadamia nut tart...131
49. Blackberry cream nut tart...134
50. Carrot-nut tart..137
51. Caramel-nut tart...139
52. Nut fruit tarts...142
53. Orange brazil nut tart...144
54. Pine nut tart...147
FRUIT TARTS..149
55. Almond-apricot tarts..150
56. Alsatian plum tart..152
57. Apple tart..154
58. Apple and raisin tarte tatin..156
59. Apple cinnamon tart..158
60. Apple cranberry upside-down tart...............................160
61. Apple raspberry tart..162
62. Blueberry buttermilk tart...165
63. Mixed fruit tart..168
64. Holiday fruit tarts..170
65. Rainbow fruit tart..172
66. Vanilla cream fruit tart..175
67. Parisienne fruit tart...177
68. Premier white fruit tart...180
VEGETABLE TART..182
69. Alpine potato tart..183
70. Artichoke tart..185

71. Pumpkin pie cheesecake Tart..188
72. Roast vegetable tarts...190
73. Roasted vegetable and goats cheese brioche tart.........192
74. Savory vegetable tart..195
75. Vegetable custard tart..198
CHEESE TARTS...201
76. Alsatian cheese tart..202
77. Amaretto cheesecake tarts...204
78. Belgian cheese tart...206
79. Bell pepper and cheese tart...208
80. Breakfast cheese tart..211
81. Creamy garlic and cheese tart...214
82. Curry and chutney cheese tart..216
83. French cheese tart..218
84. Goat cheese and spinach tart...221
85. Golden pineapple-cheese tart..223
86. Grape and currant tart with fontina cheese...................226
87. Herbed cheese tarts..228
88. Mediterranean cheese tart...231
89. Lemon-cheese tarts..234
90. Papaya-cream cheese tart with macadamia nuts.........236
91. Ricotta cheese and spinach tart..239
92. Southwest cheese tart..241
MUSHROOM TART..243
93. Exotic mushroom tart..244
94. Flaky mushroom tarts...247
95. Grilled eggplant and mushroom tart...............................249

96. Mushroom phyllo tarts..252
97. Smoky mushroom tart..254
98. Triple mushroom tart...257
99. Wild mushroom and goat's cheese tart........................259
100. Wild mushroom and pecorino tart............................262
CONCLUSION...264

INTRODUCTION

Welcome! This cookbook is designed to ignite your passion for creating delectable tarts and tartlets that will impress both family and friends. Whether you're an experienced baker or just starting out on your culinary journey, this book will guide you through the art of making irresistible pastries from scratch.

In these pages, you will find a treasure trove of recipes, carefully curated to offer a diverse range of flavors and styles. From classic fruit tarts bursting with seasonal produce to savory tartlets brimming with gourmet ingredients, there's something to please every palate. Our goal is to provide you with the knowledge and techniques necessary to achieve perfectly baked, golden crusts and luscious fillings that will have everyone coming back for more.

Each recipe is accompanied by step-by-step instructions, helpful tips, and beautiful photographs to inspire and guide you along the way. You'll learn how to master the art of creating a flaky and buttery crust, explore various filling options, and experiment with unique flavor combinations that will elevate your tart-making skills to new heights.

Whether you're hosting an elegant dinner party, preparing a special dessert for a loved one, or simply indulging in a sweet treat for yourself, the recipes in this cookbook will transform your baking endeavors into memorable culinary experiences. So, grab your rolling pin, dust off your apron, and let's embark on a delightful journey through the world of tarts and tartlets!

CRUST AND SHELLS

1. **Basic Flaky Pie Crust**

Makes: 1 tart shell

INGREDIENTS:
- 8 tablespoons unsalted butter, cold
- 1 ⅓ cups + 4 tablespoons pastry flour
- ¼ teaspoon salt
- 2 ½ to 3 ½ tablespoons of ice water
- 1 ½ teaspoons cider vinegar Optional
- ⅛ teaspoon baking powder

INSTRUCTIONS:
a) Divide the butter into two parts, about two-thirds to one-third.
b) Cut the butter into ¾-inch cubes.
c) Wrap each portion of butter with plastic wrap, refrigerate the larger amount, and freeze the smaller for at least 30 minutes.
d) Place the flour, salt, and baking powder in a gallon-size freezer bag and freeze for at least 30 minutes.
e) Add the larger amount of butter cubes to the flour and process for about 20 seconds or until the mixture resembles a coarse meal.
f) Add the remaining frozen butter cubes and pulse until all of the frozen butter is the size of peas.
g) Add the lowest amount of the ice water and the vinegar and pulse 6 times. Pinch a small amount of the mixture together between your fingers.
h) For tiny 1-inch tartlets, omit the baking powder and allow the processing to continue just until the ball forms.
i) Spoon the mixture into the plastic bag.
j) Holding both ends of the bag opening with your fingers, knead the mixture by alternately pressing it, from the outside of the bag, with the knuckles and heels of your hands until the mixture holds together in one piece and feels slightly stretchy when pulled.
k) Wrap the dough with plastic wrap, flatten it into a disc, and refrigerate for at least 45 minutes.

2. The Unshrinkable Sweet Tart Shell

Makes: enough for one 9-inch tart crust

INGREDIENTS:
- 1 ½ cups all-purpose flour
- ½ cup confectioner's sugar
- ¼ teaspoon salt
- 1 stick plus 1 tablespoon unsalted butter, cut into small pieces
- 1 large egg

INSTRUCTIONS:
a) Pulse the flour, sugar, and salt together in the bowl of a food processor. Scatter the pieces of butter over the dry ingredients and pulse until the butter is coarsely cut in.
b) Stir the yolk, just to break it up, and add it a little at a time, pulsing after each addition.
c) When the egg is in, process in long pulses—about 10 seconds each—until the dough, which will look granular soon after the egg is added, forms clumps and curds. Just before you reach this stage, the sound of the machine working the dough will change—heads up.
d) Turn the dough out onto a work surface and, very lightly and sparingly, knead the dough just to incorporate any dry ingredients that might have escaped mixing. Chill the dough, wrapped in plastic, for about 2 hours before rolling.
e) To roll the dough: Butter a 9-inch fluted tart pan with a removable bottom.
f)
g) Roll out chilled dough on a floured sheet of parchment paper to a 12-inch round, lifting and turning the dough occasionally to free it from the paper.
h) Using paper as an aid, turn the dough into a 9-inch-diameter tart pan with removable bottom; peel off the paper.
i) Seal any cracks in the dough.
j) Trim overhang to ½ inch. Fold the overhang in, making double-thick sides.

k) Pierce the crust all over with a fork.
l) Alternately, you can press the dough in as soon as it is processed: Press it evenly across the bottom and up the sides of the tart shell.
m) Freeze the crust for at least 30 minutes.
n) To fully or partially bake the crust: Center a rack in the oven and preheat the oven to 375 degrees F. Butter the shiny side of a piece of aluminum foil and fit the foil, buttered side down, tightly against the crust.
o) And here is the very best part: Since you froze the crust, you can bake it without weights. Put the tart pan on a baking sheet and bake the crust for 20 to 25 minutes.
p) Carefully remove the foil. If the crust has puffed, press it down gently with the back of a spoon.
q) Bake the crust about 10 minutes longer to fully bake it, or until it is firm and golden brown.
r) Transfer the pan to a rack and cool the crust to room temperature.

3. Cheese tart shells

Makes: 4 servings

INGREDIENTS:
- ½ cup Vegetable Shortening
- 5 ounces American Cheese Spread;1 Jar
- 1½ cups Unbleached Flour

INSTRUCTIONS:
a) Combine the shortening and cheese spread in a bowl.
b) Cut flour into the cheese mixture with two knives until well blended.
c) Shape into a roll 1¼-inch in diameter and 12 inches long.
d) Wrap completely in waxed paper or plastic wrap.
e) Refrigerate for 1 hour or longer. Preheat oven to 375 degrees F.
f) Remove the dough from the refrigerator and unwrap it. Slice ⅛-inch thick.
g) Using 12 muffin cups or 3-inch tart pans, place 1 slice of the dough in the bottom of each.
h) Overlap 5 slices around the outside of each.
i) Gently press them together. Pierce the bottoms and sides with a fork.
j) Bake for 18 to 20 minutes in the preheated oven until lightly browned.
k) Cool in the pans on a rack and gently remove the shells when cold to the touch.

4. Cornmeal crust tart shell

Makes: 1 serving

INGREDIENTS:
- 2½ cup cornmeal flour
- 1 teaspoon salt
- 1 stick cold unsalted butter; cut into pieces
- 6 tablespoons solid vegetable shortening; cold
- 5 tablespoon ice water

INSTRUCTIONS:
a) Combine the flour and salt in a bowl. Using your hands work the butter and shortening into the flour until the mixture resembles coarse crumbs. Sprinkle the ice water over the mixture 1 or 2 tablespoons at a time. Gather the dough into a ball. Turn the dough onto a floured surface.

b) Using the heel of your hand knead the dough, this will blend the butter and shortening and make the pastry flakier. Refrigerate for 30 minutes. Roll the dough out onto a floured surface into a circle 14 inches in diameter and ⅛-inch thick.

c) Gently fold the circle of the dough in half and then in half again so that you can lift it without tearing it, and unfold it into a 9-inch tart pan.

5. Free-form tart shells

Makes: 4 servings

INGREDIENTS:
- 1 egg mixed with 1 teaspoon of water
- ¼ cup granulated sugar
- 1 cup flour
- ¼ teasp0ons salt
- ⅛ teaspoons baking powder
- 8 Tablespoons unsalted butter

INSTRUCTIONS:
a) In a food processor, combine the sugar, flour, salt, and baking powder.
b) When well combined, add the butter and pulse the machine until the butter is broken up into the flour mixture.
c) Add the egg and water and process until the dough forms a dough.
d) Transfer the dough to waxed paper; pat it into a flat round and refrigerate for 30 to 45 minutes or until it has relaxed and you can roll it out.
e) Divide the dough into approximately 8 equal pieces.
f) On a lightly floured board roll out the pieces.
g) Rather than bother fitting them into tartlet shells and prebaking them, simply shape them into rough rounds or cut them into hearts or rectangles.
h) Transfer the free-form shapes to a baking sheet and chill for 20 minutes while you preheat the oven to 400 degrees.
i) Prick the dough with a fork so the dough doesn't puff up.
j) Bake for 10 to 12 minutes or until the edges are brown.
k) Remove them from the oven to a rack and let them cool.
l) When completely cool top it with whatever you like.

6. Chocolate crust

Makes: 1 Pie Crust

INGREDIENTS:
- ¾ serving Chocolate Crumb
- 8 g sugar
- 0.5 g kosher salt
- 14 g butter, melted

INSTRUCTIONS:
a) Pulse the chocolate crumbs in a food processor until they are sandy and no sizeable clusters remain.
b) Transfer the sand to a bowl and, with your hands, toss with the sugar and salt.
c) Add the melted butter and knead it into the sand until it is moist enough to knead into a ball.
d) Transfer the mixture to a 10-inch pie tin.
e) With your fingers and the palms of your hands, press the chocolate crust firmly into the tin, making sure the bottom and sides of the pie tin are evenly covered.
f) Wrapped in plastic wrap, the crust can be stored at room temp for up to 5 days or in the fridge for 2 weeks.

7. Graham crust

Makes: 2 Cups

INGREDIENTS:
- 190 g graham cracker crumbs
- 20 g milk powder
- 25 g sugar
- 3 g kosher salt
- 55 g butter, melted
- 55 g heavy cream

INSTRUCTIONS:
a) Toss the graham crumbs, milk powder, sugar, and salt with your hands in a bowl to evenly distribute your dry ingredients.
b) Whisk the butter and heavy cream together.
c) Add to the dry ingredients and toss again to evenly distribute.

8. Mini Tart Shells

Makes: 20-22 mini shells

INGREDIENTS:
- 3 cups all-purpose flour
- ⅛ teaspoon salt
- 1 ¼ cups powdered sugar
- 3 egg yolks
- 2 teaspoons vanilla bean paste or vanilla extract
- 2 sticks of unsalted butter

INSTRUCTIONS:
a) Sift flour and salt. Set aside.
b) In the mixer fitted with a petal attachment beat unsalted, room-temperature butter and powdered sugar until smooth.
c) In a small dish whisk together egg yolks and vanilla bean paste or vanilla extract.
d) Gradually beat the egg yolk mixture into the creamed butter.
e) Scrape the bowl a few times as needed.
f) On low speed, gradually add the flour mixture to the butter mixture.
g) Mix until it starts to come together. If the dough is too crumbly, add 1 teaspoon of milk.
h) Invert the dough onto a clean work surface or into a bowl and gather the dough together with your hands into a ball.
i) Then form the dough into a disk, wrap it in the foil, and chill for 1 to 2 hours
j) Preheat oven to 350F.
k) Place mini tart shell molds onto a baking sheet. Spray with a no-stick spray, and set aside.
l) Take out the chilled dough, and cut it in half. Let it soften for 5 minutes.
m) Roll it out between 2 sheets of parchment or use Dough EZ Mat.
n) Roll it out using ⅛ inch rolling guides.
o) Cut out as many rounds as you can. Gather scraps and re-roll.

p) Shape the tarts and use a fork to prick the bottom of the shells.
q) Bake at 350F for 12-14 minutes until golden around the edges.

9. French Sweet Tart Crust

Makes: 1 tart shell

INGREDIENTS:
- 1 ½ cups flour, plain/all-purpose
- 6 ½ tablespoons soft icing sugar
- 2 ½ tablespoons almond meal
- ¼ teaspoon salt
- 100g / 7 tablespoons butter, unsalted, softened, cut
- 1 large egg, at room temperature

INSTRUCTIONS:
a) Whisk together flour, icing sugar, salt, and almond meal in a bowl.
b) Use your fingertips to rub the butter into the dry ingredients until it resembles breadcrumbs.
c) Mix with a rubber spatula until it becomes too hard to stir anymore, then use your hands to bring it together into a dough.
d) Turn the dough out onto a work surface, then knead to bring it together into a smooth ball.
e) Flatten into a 2cm / 0.8" thick disc. Wrap with cling wrap and refrigerate for 30 minutes.
f) Unwrap chilled dough. Place on a lightly floured work surface.
g) Roll out into a 13-inch round.
h) Roll pastry lightly onto a rolling pin. Then unroll it gently over the tart tin.
i) Adjust the pastry to fit into the tart tin, fitting into the corner, taking care not to stretch it.
j) Roll the rolling pin over the tart tin to trim the excess dough.
k) Prick the base of the pastry 30 times with a fork.
l) Chill pastry in the tart tin for 30 minutes.

10. Cream Cheese Tart Shells

Makes: 24

INGREDIENTS:
- 3 ounces cream cheese, softened
- ½ cup butter softened
- 1 cup all-purpose flour

INSTRUCTIONS:
a) Blend cream cheese and butter or margarine. Stir in flour just until blended. Chill for about 1 hour.
b) Preheat oven to 325 degrees F.
c) Shape dough into 24 one-inch balls and press into ungreased 1 ½-inch muffin cups to make a shallow shell.
d) Fill with your favorite filling and bake for 20 minutes, or until the crust is light brown.

11. Walnut Tartlet Shells

Makes: 12

INGREDIENTS:
- 2 cups all-purpose flour, plus more for rolling out dough
- ¼ teaspoon salt
- ½ cup walnuts
- ¾ cup unsalted butter, chilled and cut into small pieces

INSTRUCTIONS:
a) Place flour, salt, and walnuts in the bowl of a food processor.
b) Pulse until the walnuts are small, but not fine.
c) Add butter, and pulse until the mixture resembles small peas, about 15 seconds.
d) With the machine running, add ¼ cup of ice water through the feed tube.
e) Pulse until the dough just starts to come together when you press it with your fingers.
f) Form dough into a ball. Flatten into a disk, and wrap in plastic.
g) Transfer to the refrigerator, and chill for at least 1 hour.
h) Set twenty-four 2-inch tartlet pans on a baking sheet.
i) Lightly dust a clean work surface with flour. Roll out dough to an ⅛-inch thickness. Using a paring knife, cut the pastry into twenty-four squares slightly larger than the pans.
j) Press dough into pans, and trim overhanging dough.
k) Place a second tartlet pan on top of each lined pan, weighing down the pastry.
l) Chill for 30 minutes more.
m) Heat oven to 375 degrees.
n) Bake the shells until lightly browned on the edges, about 10 minutes.
o) Remove top pans, and continue baking until cooked through and browned all over, 12 to 15 minutes more.
p) Turn out shells, and transfer them to wire racks to cool. Store shells in an airtight container for up to 3 days.

12. Phyllo Tart Shells

Makes: 12

INGREDIENTS:
- 1 roll of frozen phyllo dough thawed
- ½ stick butter, melted

INSTRUCTIONS:
a) Preheat oven to 375.
b) lay out phyllo dough on a cutting board. Use a pizza wheel to cut it into six squares.
c) Cover with a damp paper towel.
d) Brush the inside of two muffin tins with melted butter.
e) Uncover 1 stack of squares.
f) Brush one sheet with melted butter and lay it into a muffin tin and pat down.
g) Repeat this with five sheets.
h) Bake in a 375-degree oven for 8 minutes or until golden brown.

13. Shortbread Tart Crust

Makes: One 10-Inch Tart Crust

INGREDIENTS:
FOR THE DOUGH
- 12 tablespoons cold butter, diced
- ⅔ cup powdered sugar
- 2 egg yolks
- 2 cups all-purpose flour

FOR THE EGG WASH
- 1 egg
- 1 tablespoon water

INSTRUCTIONS:
a) Place the butter, powdered sugar, and egg yolks in the bowl of a food processor fitted with the blade.
b) Pulse until combined but still speckled with butter.
c) Add the flour and run the machine just until the dough comes together when you pinch it between your fingers.
d) Turn the dough out onto a large piece of parchment, knead a few times to bring it all together, and pat it into a disc shape.
e) Wrap well in the parchment and chill for about half an hour.
f) Preheat the oven to 350°F with a rack in the center.
g) Remove the dough from the fridge and let it rest on the counter for 15 minutes.
h) Sprinkle a bit of flour on your work surface and over the surface of the dough.
i) Roll out the dough with a rolling pin to an approximately 12-inch circle.
j) Transfer the dough very carefully to a 10-inch tart pan with a removable bottom, pressing on the dough lightly so it sits snugly against the bottom and sides of the pan.
k) Prick the bottom of the shell all over with a fork. Place the whole thing onto a baking sheet.
l) Place a piece of parchment paper over the shell, making sure to cover the edges.

m) Spread plenty of dried beans or pie weights over the parchment, covering the whole bottom of the tart shell.
n) Bake for 15 minutes this way, then remove the parchment and beans.
o) Brush the shell with a bit of egg wash.
p) Return the shell to the oven for at least an additional 10 minutes.
q) Remove from the oven and cool completely before filling.

14. Eggless Tart Crust

Makes: 9.5-inch tart crust

INGREDIENTS:
- 1 ¼ cup 175 g all-purpose flour
- ⅓ cup 40 g confectioners' sugar
- ¼ teaspoon kosher salt
- ½ cup 115 g unsalted butter, cold and diced
- 1 tablespoon 15 ml evaporated milk
- 2 teaspoons 10 ml heavy cream
- 1 teaspoon 5 ml pure vanilla extract

INSTRUCTIONS:
Make the Dough:
a) Place the flour, sugar, and salt in the bowl of a food processor, stand mixer, or bowl; pulse to combine.
b) Add the chopped butter and process in short bursts until the mixture resembles coarse meal or fine breadcrumbs.
c) With the motor running, add the evaporated milk, cream, and vanilla, and process/mix/stir until the dough comes together into a ball and pulls away cleanly from the sides of the bowl.
d) By Hand: Mix dry ingredients in a big bowl.
e) Use a pastry cutter or two knives, to cut the butter into the flour mixture until the texture resembles coarse cornmeal.
f) And then, add wet ingredients and mix with a fork just until the dough comes together.
g) Turn the dough onto a lightly floured surface.
h) Bring the dough together and flatten it into a dish shape. Wrap in plastic wrap and refrigerate for 1 hour.
i) On a lightly floured surface, roll the dough.
j) Flour the rolling pin, roll the dough loosely around it, and then unroll it into the tart pan.
k) Use your fingers to drape it in and gently pat the dough onto the bottom and sides of the tart pan evenly instead of pulling or stretching it.
l) Seal any cracks in the dough, if needed.

m) Trim off excess dough with a sharp knife or with the rolling pin by rolling over the tart pan.
n) With a fork, gently prick the base several times.
o) Cover the tart pan with plastic wrap and place in the freezer until firm, about 30 minutes.
p) Preheat oven to 400º F.
q) Line chilled tart crust with a double layer of parchment paper or aluminum foil.
r) Fill the crust with pie weights.

BAKE:
s) Bake at 400º F for 15 – 18 minutes, or until the edges are set, and the paper/foil no longer sticks to the dough.
t) Remove the tart crust from the oven. Remove weights and paper.
u) To partially bake the crust: After removing the weights, bake for 5 minutes longer.
v) To fully bake the crust: After removing the weights, bake for about 10 – 12 minutes longer, or until golden and crisp.
w) Transfer to a wire rack and let cool completely before filling.

15. Whole Wheat Tart Crust

Makes: 9-inch tart crust

INGREDIENTS:
- ¾ cup margarine
- 1 ½ cups whole wheat flour
- ½ teaspoon salt
- 4 tablespoons ice water, or as needed

INSTRUCTIONS:
a) Preheat the oven to 350 degrees F.
b) Place margarine in a stainless steel bowl.
c) Mix using an electric mixer fitted with a paddle attachment on low speed until slightly soft.
d) Pour in flour and salt; continue to mix at low speed to combine.
e) Pour in ice water gradually until a dough forms.
f) Divide dough in half. Wrap one portion of the dough in plastic and refrigerate for later use.
g) Roll out the other portion of the dough on a lightly floured surface with a lightly floured rolling pin.
h) Mold into a 9-inch tart pan. Prick the dough base evenly with a fork.
i) Bake in the preheated oven until the crust is lightly browned, 10 to 15 minutes.

CHOCOLATE TARTS

16. Truffle tart with espresso sauce

Makes: 1 serving

INGREDIENTS:
- 1½ cups Chocolate Wafer crumbs
- 6 tablespoons Sweet Butter

FILLING:
- 12 ounces Semi-Sweet Chocolate
- ½ cup Heavy cream
- 1 Stick sweet butter,
- Cut into bits and softened
- 2 tablespoons Kahlua Liqueur
- 1 Pinch salt

SAUCE:
- ½ cup Whipping cream
- 4 tablespoons Sugar
- ¼ cup Butter
- 1 teaspoon Finely ground Expresso
- 1 teaspoon Coffee

INSTRUCTIONS:

a) Crush or grind fine chocolate wafers in a food processor. Melt butter and blend into crumbs. Pat into tart or pie pan. Chill until firm before filling or bake at 300 degrees for 15 minutes, cool, and fill.

b) Filling: In a large saucepan combine the chocolate, cream, butter, and Kahlua and heat the mixture over moderately low heat, stirring until it is smooth. Remove from heat, and allow to cool for 30 minutes at room temperature.

c) Pour into the cooled tart shell and refrigerate for at least 3 hours.

d) Sauce: In a saucepan, combine cream, sugar, and butter. Cook over low heat, stirring frequently until the mixture boils. Boil for 5 minutes, stirring occasionally. Remove from heat. Stir in expresso grounds.

e) To serve, spoon a moderate amount of warm sauce on a rimmed plate. Top with a wedge of the tart.

17. Dark Chocolate Tart with Gingersnap Crust

Makes: 10 servings

CRUST:
- 8 ounces gingersnap cookies, coarsely broken
- ¼ cup salted butter, melted

FILLING:
- 12 ounces bittersweet chocolate, finely chopped
- 1 cup heavy whipping cream
- 2 large egg yolks
- 1 large egg
- ¼ cup sugar
- 1 tablespoon all-purpose flour
- ⅛ teaspoon freshly ground black pepper
- Pinch of salt
- ¼ teaspoon cinnamon
- Softly whipped cream, for serving

INSTRUCTIONS:
FOR CRUST:
a) Preheat oven to 325°F. Finely grind gingersnap cookies in the processor.
b) Add melted butter and process until moistened.
c) Press the crumb mixture firmly onto the bottom and upsides of a 9-inch-diameter tart pan with removable bottom.
d) Place the pan on the rimmed baking sheet.

FOR FILLING:
e) Combine finely chopped bittersweet chocolate and heavy whipping cream in a heavy medium saucepan.
f) Whisk over low heat until the chocolate is melted and smooth.
g) Remove the saucepan from the heat.
h) Whisk egg yolks, egg, sugar, flour, ground black pepper, salt, and cinnamon in a bowl to blend.
i) Very gradually whisk the chocolate mixture into the egg mixture until smooth and blended.
j) Pour chocolate filling into the crust.

k) Bake chocolate tart until filling puffs slightly at the edges and the center is softly set about 30 minutes. Transfer to rack. Cool tart in pan for 20 minutes.

l) Gently remove tart pan sides and cool tart completely.

m) Cut tart into thin wedges and serve with softly whipped cream.

18. Chocolate brownie tart

Makes: 10 servings

INGREDIENTS:
- 1 cup flour
- ¼ cup Firmly packed light brown sugar
- 1-ounce Chocolate; unsweetened, grated
- ½ cup Butter; cut into ½ inch pieces, well chilled
- 2 tablespoons Milk
- 1 teaspoon Vanilla
- 3 ounces of Unsweetened chocolate
- 3 ounces Semisweet chocolate
- ½ cup Butter; room temperature, cut into pieces
- 1½ cup Sugar
- 3 Eggs; beaten to blend
- 2 teaspoons Vanilla
- ½ cup Chopped walnuts
- ¾ cup All-purpose flour
- 4 ounces Semi-sweet chocolate; melted
- ¼ Butter; room temperature
- 2 teaspoons Vegetable oil

INSTRUCTIONS:
FOR PASTRY:
a) Combine flour, brown sugar, and grated chocolate in a bowl. Cut in butter until the mixture resembles a coarse meal. Mix in milk and vanilla with a fork until just blended. Pat pastry into bottom and sides of 11-inch tart pan, flouring fingertips as needed if mixture becomes too sticky.

FOR FILLING:
b) Preheat oven to 350 degrees. Melt the chocolates on top of a double boiler set over hot water. Remove from heat and stir in butter one piece at a time.

c) Transfer the mixture to a bowl. Add sugar and blend well; the mixture will be granular.

d) Add beaten eggs, a third at a time, blending well after each addition. Mix in vanilla. Stir in chopped nuts.
e) Gradually add flour, blending well after each addition. Pour into pastry shell.
f) Bake until the center is just set and a tester inserted in the center comes out clean, 20 to 25 minutes.
g) Let tart cool on a wire rack.

FOR ICING:
h) Combine chocolate, butter, and oil in a bowl and mix until smooth.
i) Cool to a spreadable consistency, whisking occasionally.
j) Spread icing over the top of the tart. Let stand until the icing sets.
k) Cut into wedges to serve.

19. Chocolate butter tarts

Makes: 12 Tarts

INGREDIENTS:
- 3 squares of bittersweet chocolate
- 12 Unbaked med. tart shells
- ¾ cup Lightly packed brown sugar
- ¼ cup Corn syrup
- 1 Egg
- 2 tablespoons Butter; softened
- 1 teaspoon Vanilla
- 1 teaspoon Vinegar
- pinch Salt
- 1 Square bittersweet chocolate melted

INSTRUCTIONS:
a) Chop each of the three squares of chocolate into 16 pieces.
b) Place 4 chunks into the bottom of each tart shell. Whisk together brown sugar, corn syrup, egg, butter, vanilla, vinegar, and salt. Spoon into tart shells, filling three-quarters full.
c) Bake at 450 degrees for 12-14 minutes, or until the filling is puffed and bubbly and the pastry is lightly golden. Let cool on racks.
d) Drizzle with melted chocolate.

20. Chocolate coconut mini tarts

Makes: 36 servings

INGREDIENTS:
- 14 oz sweetened condensed Milk
- 2 tablespoons Hazelnut liqueur or water
- 2 tablespoons Water
- 1 pack of instant chocolate

PUDDING MIX
- 13 ¾oz package of soft macaroons
- 1 cup Finely chopped pecans
- 2 tablespoons Unsweetened cocoa powder
- ⅔ cup Whipping cream

COCONUT CRUSTS
- Toasted coconut, optional
- Whipped cream, optional
- ⅓ cup Butter or margarine, melted

INSTRUCTIONS:
a) Combine sweetened condensed milk, liqueur, or water and water.
b) Add pudding mix and cocoa powder. Beat until smooth.
c) Cover and chill for 5 minutes.
d) Beat ⅔ cup whipping cream to soft peaks; fold into the chocolate mixture.
e) Mound into coconut crusts. Chill for 2 to 24 hours.
f) Garnish with additional whipped cream and toasted coconut if desired.

COCONUT CRUSTS:
g) Mix macaroons, pecans, and butter.
h) Press 1 tablespoon mixture into the bottom and up sides of 36 well-greased 1¾" muffin cups.
i) Bake in a 375-degree oven for 8-10 minutes or till the edges are browned. Cool on rack.
j) Loosen; remove from cups.

21. Chocolate hazelnut tart

Makes: 8 servings

INGREDIENTS:
- 3 tablespoons Cocoa powder
- ¼ cup Sugar
- 4 tablespoons Butter
- 1 Egg
- 4 ounces Bittersweet or semisweet chocolate
- ¼ t baking soda
- 4 tablespoons Butter
- 1 cup Dark corn syrup
- ½ cup Sugar
- 3 Eggs
- 2 tablespoons Dark rum

CHOCOLATE DOUGH
- 1 cup Unbleached all-purpose
- Pinch salt

FILLING
- 2 cups whole Hazelnuts

INSTRUCTIONS:
a) Sift the dry ingredients together three times.
b) Rub in the butter and moisten with the egg.
c) Shape into a disk, wrap, and refrigerate. Cooking the Chocolate-Hazelnut Filling.
d) Place the hazelnuts on a baking pan and toast at 350 degrees F until the skins are loose and come off easily about 10 minutes. Rub the hazelnuts in a towel to remove the skins.
e) Chop the hazelnuts coarsely, by hand, or with a food processor. Combine the chocolate with the butter in a bowl. Bring a small pan of water to a simmer and turn off the heat.
f) Place the bowl of chocolate and butter over the hot water and stir to melt. Combine the corn syrup and sugar in a pan. Bring to a full rolling boil over medium heat.

g) Remove from heat and stir in the chocolate mixture. Beat the eggs and salt with the optional rum. Beat in the chocolate mixture, taking care not to overbeat. Assembling.

h) Lightly flour the work surface and dough. Roll the dough to a 14-inch diameter disk, ⅛ inch thick.

i) Line a 10-inch tart pan with the dough, trimming away the excess.

j) Stir the chipped hazelnuts into the filling and pour the filling into the pan. Baking. Bake at 350 degrees F until the filling is set and the crust is baked through about 40 minutes. Holding. Store the tart at room temperature for up to 2 days.

22. Chocolate mascarpone nut tart

Makes: 1 serving

INGREDIENTS:
- 1 cup All-purpose flour
- ¾ cup Granulated sugar
- ½ teaspoon Salt
- 1 cup Unsweetened alkalized cocoa powder
- 6 ounces Chilled unsalted butter cut into ½-inch pieces
- 4 large Egg yolks
- 6 ounces Bittersweet chocolate; finely chopped
- 1 cup Sour cream
- 1 cup Heavy cream
- ½ cup Granulated sugar; divided
- 2 large Eggs
- 4 large Egg yolks
- 2 teaspoons Cornstarch
- 8 ounces Mascarpone cheese
- ¾ cup Heavy cream
- 4 ounces Chestnut puree
- ½ cup Confectioners' sugar
- 1 teaspoon Vanilla extract

INSTRUCTIONS:
a) In a food processor fitted with a metal chopping blade, combine the flour, sugar, salt, and cocoa powder. Pulse the machine eight to nine times to blend. Scatter the butter over the flour mixture and pulse the machine until the butter is cut into the flour and the mixture resembles a coarse meal.

b) Add the yolks and continue to process in on/off pulses only until the mixture is evenly incorporated and the particles begin to hold together. Scrape the dough onto a work surface and form it into a ball. Flatten it into a disc and wrap it in plastic wrap. Chill for 1 hour.

c) Position a rack in the center of the oven and preheat to 350 degrees F.

d) Remove the chilled disc from the refrigerator. Place the dough between two pieces of plastic wrap and roll the dough into a small round. Lift and rotate the dough one-quarter turn after each roll. Continue rolling until the circle measures approximately 14 inches in diameter and is about ⅛ inch thick. Remove the top layer of plastic wrap.

e) Carefully roll the dough around the rolling pin and transfer it to a 12-inch fluted tart pan with a removable bottom. Unroll the dough into the pan. Lift the edges of the dough and gently press the dough into the bottom and up the sides of the pan. Trim off any excess dough. Refrigerate the dough for 20 to 30 minutes, until firm.

f) Bake the tart shell for 20 to 30 minutes or until set. Place on a wire rack and cool completely.

CHOCOLATE CREAM:

g) Place the chopped chocolate in a bowl and set aside.

h) In a non-corrosive medium saucepan bring the sour cream, heavy cream, and ¼ cup of sugar to a boil over medium-high heat.

i) In a bowl using a hand-held electric mixer, beat the eggs, egg yolks, cornstarch, and the remaining ¼ cup of sugar at medium speed until pale. Whisk one-third of the hot cream mixture into the egg mixture and return the whole mixture to the pan.

j) Cook over medium-high heat while constantly stirring with a whisk for 3 to 5 minutes or until thick. Pour the thickened mixture over the reserved chocolate and whisk until incorporated.

k) Scrape the mixture into the prepared crust and smooth the top with a rubber spatula. Chill in the refrigerator for 2 hours.

MASCARPONE TOPPING:

l) In a 4½-quart bowl of a heavy-duty electric mixer, using the wire whip attachment, combine the mascarpone, heavy cream, chestnut puree, confectioners' sugar, and vanilla.

m) Beat on medium-high speed until soft peaks form. Place the mixture in a pastry bag fitted with a medium star tip and pipe in a shell pattern covering the top of the chilled tart.

n) Refrigerate the tart for 1 hour before serving.

23. Chocolate miniature tarts

Makes: 50 servings

INGREDIENTS:
- 2¼ cup All-purpose flour
- ¾ cup Margarine
- ⅓ cup Confectioner's sugar
- ⅔ cup Semisweet chocolate chips
- 2 tablespoons Margarine
- ½ cup Sugar
- ½ cup Corn syrup
- 2 Eggs
- ¼ cup Pecans, chopped
- 1 cup Dried coconut

INSTRUCTIONS:
a) Mix flour, ¾ cup margarine, and powdered sugar. Press about 1 teaspoon of pastry evenly against the bottoms and sides of ungreased tiny muffin cups.
b) Melt chocolate chips and 2 tablespoons of margarine in a double boiler over simmering water until chips and margarine are melted; remove from heat.
c) Mix in sugar and syrup; beat in eggs.
d) Spoon 1 to 2 teaspoons of the chocolate mixture into each tart shell, and fill to ¾ full only.
e) Sprinkle with pecans and coconut.
f) Bake in preheated 350-degree oven for 20 to 25 minutes.
g) Cool for a few minutes.
h) Carefully remove from muffin cups with the tip of a knife. Cool completely. Top with sweetened whipped cream if desired.

24. Chocolate truffle tart with raspberries

Makes: 6 Servings

INGREDIENTS:
- 1 cup Flour, all-purpose
- ½ cup Sugar, granulated
- ½ cup Cocoa powder
- 3 ounces Butter; chilled
- 1 Egg
- 6 ounces Semisweet chocolate; chopped
- 2 cups Whipping cream
- 3-4 cups raspberries

INSTRUCTIONS:
CHOCOLATE PASTRY:
a) Combine flour, sugar, and cocoa in the bowl of a food processor.
b) Pulse 2 or 3 times to aerate. Chop the butter into pieces and distribute over the flour.
c) With the motor running, drop in the whole egg through the feed tube.
d) Process very briefly - do not let the dough come together or your pastry will be tough.
e) Remove the dough from the work bowl and set aside at room temperature until the filling is made.

TRUFFLE FILLING:
f) Place the chopped chocolate in a medium-sized bowl, and bring the cream to boil over medium-high heat.
g) Pour over the chocolate and whisk till all the chocolate is melted. Cover with plastic wrap and refrigerate until set.
h) Preheat the oven to 375F. Work the chocolate pastry with your hands and press it into a tart pan with removable bottom; try to get an even thickness. Chill for 20 minutes. Prick the bottom of the pastry with a fork.
i) Bake in preheated oven for 20 to 25 minutes. Cool completely. TO

ASSEMBLE:
j) Remove the tart gently form the pan and set it on a platter. Spoon over pipe the truffle filling into the shell and smooth the surface. Arrange the raspberries over the top in concentric circles.

25. Cranberry and white chocolate tart

Makes: 1 Serving

INGREDIENTS:
- 2½ cups Cranberries; fresh or frozen and defrosted
- ¼ cup Fresh orange juice
- ½ cup Sugar
- 1 cup Ground blanched almonds
- 1⅔ cup Unbleached all-purpose flour
- ½ cup Sugar
- ½ teaspoon Baking powder
- 1 teaspoon Ground cinnamon
- ¼ teaspoon Ground mace
- ½ pounds Cold unsalted butter; cut into 16 pieces
- 1 large Egg
- 1 large Egg yolk
- 1 teaspoon Vanilla extract
- 6 ounces White chocolate; chopped
- Powdered sugar; for dusting

INSTRUCTIONS:
a) Cook the cranberries, orange juice, and sugar in a medium saucepan over medium heat until the mixture comes to a boil.
b) Reduce the heat to medium-low and simmer, stirring occasionally, until the liquid becomes thick and syrupy, about 10 minutes. The cranberry mixture will have a jam-like consistency. Set aside to cool thoroughly, about 30 minutes. The mixture will thicken to a firm jam when cool.
c) Position an oven rack in the middle of the oven and preheat the oven to 350 degrees. Butter a 9-inch spring-form pan.
d) In the bowl of an electric mixer combine the almonds, flour, sugar, baking powder, cinnamon, and mace. Mix on low speed just to blend the ingredients, about 10 seconds. Add the butter and mix until most of the butter pieces are the size of peas, about 1 minute. The mixture will look crumbly and the crumbs will vary in size.

e) With the mixer running, add the egg, egg yolk, and vanilla. Mix until the mixture clings together and pulls away from the sides of the bowl, about 30 seconds. Reserve 1 cup of the mixture for the lattice topping and refrigerate it while you prepare the crust.

f) Press the remaining dough evenly over the bottom and 1¼-inches up the sides of the prepared pan. Sprinkle the white chocolate evenly over the crust. Use a thin metal spatula to spread the cooled cranberry mixture evenly over the white chocolate.

g) Remove the reserved dough from the refrigerator. Using about 2 tablespoons of the dough for the longest ropes and less for the shorter ropes, roll pieces of the dough back and forth to form ropes of dough about ½-inch in diameter. If ropes break, pinch them back together.

h) Put a 9-inch long rope across the middle of the tart. Spacing the ropes about 2 inches apart, place a rope about 8 inches long on either side of the center rope. Place a rope about 4 ½-inches long near each end of the tart. You will have 5 ropes of the dough across the top of the tart.

i) Turn the tart pan a half turn and place 5 more ropes evenly over the top of the tart for a lattice pattern. Bake the tart until the top is golden brown, about 1 hour. Cool the tart thoroughly in the pan. Sprinkle with powdered sugar before serving.

26. Double chocolate cream tart

Makes: 12 Servings

INGREDIENTS:
- 1 cup All-purpose flour; divided
- ¼ cup Ice water
- 1 tablespoon Vanilla; divided
- ¾ cup unsweetened cocoa; divided
- 2 tablespoons Sugar
- ¼ teaspoon Salt
- ¼ cup Vegetable shortening
- Cooking spray
- 14 ounces can fat-free sweetened condensed milk
- 6 ounces ⅓ less fat cream cheese; softened
- 1 large Egg
- 1 large Egg white
- 1½ cups Frozen reduced-calorie whipped topping; thawed
- 1-ounce Semisweet chocolate; finely chopped

INSTRUCTIONS:
a) Preheat oven to 350°. Combine ¼ cup flour, ice water, and 1 teaspoon vanilla, stirring with a whisk until well-blended; set aside.
b) Combine ¾ cup flour, ¼ cup cocoa, sugar, and salt in a bowl; cut in shortening with a pastry blender or 2 knives until the mixture resembles a coarse meal.
c) Add ice water mixture; toss with a fork until moist and crumbly.
d) Gently press the mixture into a 4-inch circle on heavy-duty plastic wrap; cover with additional plastic wrap.
e) Roll dough, still covered, into a 13-inch circle.
f) Place dough in the freezer for 30 minutes or until plastic wrap can be easily removed.
g) Remove the top sheet of plastic wrap; fit dough, uncovered side down, into a 10-inch round removable-bottom tart pan coated with cooking spray.
h) Remove the remaining sheet of plastic wrap. Fold edges.

i) Pierce the bottom and sides of the dough with a fork; bake at 350° for 4 minutes.
j) Cool on a wire rack. Place tart pan on a baking sheet; set aside.
k) Beat ½ cup cocoa and milk at medium speed of a mixer until blended.
l) Add cheese; beat well. Add 2 teaspoons of vanilla, egg, and egg white; beat just until smooth.
m) Pour mixture into the crust; bake at 350° for 25 minutes or until set.
n) Spread whipped topping over the tart; sprinkle with chopped chocolate.

27. Fudgy chocolate tart

Makes: 12 Servings

INGREDIENTS:
- 8 ounces of Bittersweet chocolate; broken into chunks
- ⅓ cup Margarine or butter
- 2 large Eggs; at room temperature
- 1 teaspoon Vanilla extract
- ⅓ cup Granulated sugar
- ¾ cup All-purpose flour
- ¼ teaspoon Salt
- 4 ounces Mascarpone cheese; at room temperature

INSTRUCTIONS:

a) Delightfully rich, this festive dessert has a brownie-like texture accented with sweet, creamy mascarpone cheese.

b) Preheat oven to 350 degrees. Grease a 9-inch tart pan with removable bottom; set aside.

c) In a small heavy saucepan, melt chocolate and margarine over low heat, stirring frequently. Remove from heat.

d) In a bowl, beat eggs and vanilla with an electric mixer at medium speed for 30 seconds. Gradually beat in sugar; beat for 1 minute. Beat in the chocolate mixture, scraping down the sides of the bowl once. Beat in flour and salt at low speed just until blended. Spread batter evenly in the prepared pan.

e) Put cheese into a bowl and stir well with a fork. Drop by teaspoonful randomly over the surface of the chocolate batter. Using a sharp knife, swirl the cheese mixture into the chocolate mixture to create a marbling effect.

f) Bake until the center is just set, 20 to 25 minutes. Remove pan to wire rack and cool completely. Cover tart with plastic wrap; place in a large plastic freezer bag and freeze for up to 6 weeks before serving.

g) Thaw tart completely at room temperature. Remove from tart pan.

h) Cut into wedges and serve.

28. Fresh fruit and chocolate tart

Makes: 8 servings

INGREDIENTS:
- 1¼ cup Flour
- 4 ounces Stick butter; softened
- 3 tablespoons Sugar
- 1 teaspoon Vanilla extract
- ¼ cup Pecans or walnuts finely chopped
- 1 cup Milk chocolate chips
- ⅓ cup Sour cream
- Fresh fruit in season
- 3 tablespoons apricot or seedless
- Raspberry jam

INSTRUCTIONS:
a) Preheat oven to 400°F.
CRUST
In a bowl, combine flour, butter, sugar, ½ teaspoon vanilla, and pecans. Blend with a fork until the mixture resembles fine crumbs. Knead until the dough holds together.
b) Press dough firmly and evenly onto the bottom and sides of a 9½-inch fluted metal tart pan with removable bottom.
c) Bake for 14 to 16 minutes, or until golden. Let cool.
FILLING
d) In a 2-cup glass measuring cup, heat chocolate chips in the microwave on High for about 1 min, or until completely melted and smooth when stirred. Stir in sour cream and the remaining ½ teaspoon vanilla.
e) Spread the filling evenly over the cooled crust. Refrigerate for 2 to 3 hours, or overnight.
f) About 1 hour before serving, cut peaches, nectarines, kiwi, or cantaloupe into slices or crescents; drain fruit on paper towels if extremely juicy. Arrange in concentric circles or other designs on top of the chocolate filling.

g) Fill in with grapes and berries until the top is completely covered with fruit. Warm jam in a microwave or over low heat until melted. Brush jam over fruit. Refrigerate until serving time.

h) Just before serving, remove the side of the pan and set the tart on a serving dish.

29. Spicy chocolate tart

Makes: 1 serving

INGREDIENTS:
- 1 cup Unbleached all-purpose flour
- 2 tablespoons Cocoa powder
- ¼ cup Sugar
- 1 pinch Salt
- ½ teaspoon Baking powder
- 4 tablespoons Unsalted butter
- 1 large Egg
- ⅓ cup Water
- ⅓ cup Sugar
- ½ Stick unsalted butter
- 6 ounces of Semisweet chocolate
- 3 large Eggs
- 1 teaspoon Ground cinnamon
- ½ teaspoon Ground cloves

INSTRUCTIONS:
a) For the dough: Place flour in a bowl and sift the cocoa powder over it. Stir in the sugar, salt, and baking powder. Rub in the butter finely, leaving the mixture cool and powdery. Beat the egg and stir it into the dough. Press the dough together and wrap and chill it.
b) Preheat oven to 350 degrees and set the rack in the lower third of the oven. On a floured surface, roll the dough and line a buttered 10-inch tart pan. Set aside.
c) In a saucepan, over medium heat, bring sugar and water to a boil. Add butter and continue heating to melt butter. Off heat whisk in finely cut chocolate. Whisk eggs with spices, then whisk in a chocolate mixture. Pour into tart shell.
d) Bake for about 30 minutes, until well-risen and firm. Cool on a rack.
e) Unmold the tart and serve with sweetened whipped cream.

30. Strawberry white chocolate mousse tart

Makes: 8 servings

INGREDIENTS:
PASTRY:
- 1¾ cup Unbleached Flour
- ¼ cup Firmly Packed Light Brown Sugar
- 2½ teaspoon Orange Peel, grated
- ⅛ teaspoon Salt
- 1¾ Sticks Unsalted Butter
- 1½ tablespoon Fresh Orange Juice
- 1 Egg Yolk
- 1 teaspoon Vanilla Extract
- 2 ounces of White Chocolate

MOUSSE:
- 6 ounces of White Chocolate
- ¼ cup Heavy Cream
- 1 large Egg White
- 1 tablespoon Sugar
- ½ cup Whipping Cream, whipped
- 2 tablespoons Grand Marnier
- 1 large Strawberries, with stems
- 25 large Strawberries, hulled
- ½ cup Strawberry Jam

INSTRUCTIONS:
a) For the pastry: Mix the first 4 ingredients in a bowl. Add butter and cut into the mixture until it resembles a fine meal. Blend orange juice with egg yolk and vanilla. Add enough juice mixture to dry the ingredients to form a ball that comes together.

b) Gather dough into a ball and flatten it into roughly a 12-inch round.

c) Position the rack in the center of the oven and preheat to 375 degrees.

d) Roll dough out between sheets of plastic wrap to ⅛ inch thickness. Trim to an 11-inch circle.

e) Remove plastic wrap from the top and invert into a 10-inch round spring-form pan with removable bottom. Remove plastic wrap and press into the bottom and up sides of the pan... crimp the top edges.

f) Freeze for 15 minutes. Line the tart shell with aluminum foil and add pie weights or beans.

g) Bake until sides are set - about 10 minutes.

h) Remove foil and weights. Bake crust until golden brown - about 16-20 minutes.

i) Sprinkle two ounces of white chocolate over the hot crust. Let stand for about 1 minute.

j) Using the back of a spoon, spread chocolate over the bottom and sides.

k) Transfer to a rack to cool.

31. Swedish chocolate dessert konungens tarts

Makes: 6 Servings

INGREDIENTS:
- 2¼ cup Pillsbury's Best All-purpose Flour
- ½ cup Sugar
- ⅓ cup Cocoa
- ½ teaspoon Double-acting baking powder
- ½ teaspoon Salt
- ¾ cup Butter
- 1 Egg; slightly beaten
- 1 tablespoon Milk -Filling
- 1 Egg
- ¼ cup Sugar
- ¼ cup Pillsbury's Best All-purpose Flour
- 1 cup Milk
- 1 teaspoon French Vanilla
- ½ cup Whipping cream -For chocolate filling---
- 3 tablespoons Cocoa
- 3 tablespoons Sugar -Chocolate Icing---
- 2 tablespoons Butter; melted
- 2 tablespoons Cocoa
- ½ cup Confectioners' sugar
- 1 Egg yolk
- ¼ teaspoon French Vanilla

INSTRUCTIONS:
a) BAKE at 375 degrees for 12 to 15 minutes.
b) Sift together the flour, sugar, cocoa, baking powder, and salt.
c) Cut in butter until particles are the size of small peas.
d) Add 1 slightly beaten egg and 1 to tablespoons milk; blend with a fork or pastry blender.
e) Place on a large ungreased baking sheet.
f) Roll out on a baking sheet with a floured rolling pin to a 15 x 11-inch rectangle.

g) Trim edges with a knife or pastry wheel. Cut into three 11 x 5-inch rectangles.
h) Bake in a moderate oven, 375 degrees, for 12 to 15 minutes.
i) Cool on the baking sheet. Loosen carefully with a spatula.
j) Stack layers on top of cardboard covered with aluminum foil, spreading filling between layers to within ¼ inch of edge.
k) Frost top. if desired, decorate with toasted slivered almonds. Chill until the frosting has set.
l) Wrap loosely in aluminum foil; chill overnight.

FILLING:
m) Beat 1 egg until light and fluffy.
n) Gradually add sugar, beating constantly until thick and light. Blend in flour.
o) Gradually add milk that has been scalded on top of a double boiler.
p) Return mixture to double boiler. Cook over boiling water, stirring constantly, until thick and smooth. Add vanilla; cool.
q) Beat ½ cup whipping cream until thick and fold into the filling.
r) Combine ½ cup whipping cream, cocoa, and sugar. Beat until thick.

CHOCOLATE ICING:
s) Combine melted butter, cocoa, confectioners' sugar, egg yolk, and vanilla. Beat until smooth.

32. White chocolate banana crème tart

Makes: 8 servings

INGREDIENTS:
- ½ cup unsalted butter, room temperature
- 6 tablespoons Sugar
- 1 large Egg
- 1 cup Plus 6 T all-purpose flour
- 3 large Egg yolks
- 2 tablespoons Sugar
- 2 tablespoons Cornstarch
- 1 cup Milk
- ½ Vanilla bean split lengthwise
- 3 ounces Imported white chocolate finely chopped
- 1 tablespoon Unsalted butter
- ½ cup Chilled whipping cream
- 3 Bananas, peeled
- 1½ tablespoon Banana liqueur
- 1 tablespoon Fresh lemon juice
- 4 ounces Imported white chocolate, shaved with a vegetable peeler

INSTRUCTIONS:
PASTRY:
a) Using an electric mixer, beat butter and sugar in a bowl until just combined.
b) Add egg; beat until blended. Add flour and beat for 2 minutes.
c) Gather dough into a ball and flatten it into a disk.
d) Wrap in plastic and refrigerate for 3 hours.
e) Preheat oven to 375'F. Roll out dough on a floured surface to a 12-inch- diameter round.
f) Transfer to a 9-inch diameter tart pan with removable bottom.
g) Trim crust, leaving a ¼-inch overhang. Reserve pastry scraps.
h) Fold edges over to form double-thick sides. Freeze for 15 minutes. Line the pastry with foil.

i) Fill with dried beans or pie weights. Bake for 15 minutes. Remove foil and beans.
j) Repair any cracks with reserved pastry scraps. Bake until golden, about 20 minutes.
k) Cool completely.

FILLING:
l) Whisk yolks, sugar, and cornstarch in a bowl until combined.
m) Pour milk into heavy a pan. Scrape in seeds from vanilla bean; add bean.
n) Bring mixture to boil.
o) Whisk milk mixture into egg mixture.
p) Return mixture to the same saucepan and bring to a boil, whisking constantly. Strain into a bowl.
q) Add 3 ounces of chopped white chocolate and butter; stir until melted. Cover and chill for at least 3 hours.
r) Whip cream in a bowl to stiff peaks. Fold into the white chocolate pastry cream. Cut bananas into ¼-inch thick slices.
s) Transfer to a bowl; add liqueur and lemon juice and toss. Fold bananas into the pastry cream. Spoon filling into the tart shell, mounding in the center.
t) Top with chocolate shavings. Chill for at least 1 hour and up to 6 hours.

33. Wicked dark chocolate tart

Makes: 1 serving

INGREDIENTS:
- 250 grams of Unsalted butter
- 125 grams of Vanilla sugar
- 250 grams of Plain flour
- 125 grams Semolina
- 180 grams of Dark bitter chocolate
- 5 tablespoons Cognac
- 4 Eggs
- 3 tablespoons Corn flour
- 400 grams of Caster sugar
- 600 milliliters Single cream
- 1 Vanilla pod
- 125 grams of Unsalted butter

INSTRUCTIONS:
a) Preheat the oven to 180C/gas 4. Prepare the shortcake. Cream butter and vanilla sugar in a bowl until light and fluffy.
b) Mix flour and semolina. Gradually add to the butter until a crumbly dough is formed. Carefully and gently knead the dough until it binds together and the surface is smooth. Roll out thinly to line 6 loose-bottomed 4-inch tart tins. Prick bases. Chill well for an hour. Line with foil and baking beans.
c) Bake pastry cases blind for 20 minutes or so in preheated oven until cooked through. Remove beans and foil and continue drying out in the oven if necessary. Prepare chocolate filling. Break the chocolate into squares. Place in a bowl over a pan of water or a double boiler. Add cognac to chocolate.
d) Heat gently until the chocolate is melted. Beat eggs in a bowl. Blend in corn flour and sugar and add a little cream, if necessary.
e) Heat the remaining cream in a saucepan with vanilla pods until almost boiling.
f) Stir hot cream into the blended egg mixture.

g) Rinse cream pan in cold water. Return mixture to pay and add melted chocolate. Cook gently, stirring constantly, until the mixture thickens and the corn flour is cooked. Taste the mixture to check it is not floury. This will take between 6-8 minutes. Remove the vanilla pod.

h) Cool filling slightly. Soften butter and allow to cool. Beat softened butter into the chocolate filling. Pour into chilled tarts and leave to set.

i) When cold make chocolate leaves with some melted chocolate and use them to decorate the tarts.

SEAFOOD TARTS

34. Alaska seafood tarts

Makes: 6 Servings

INGREDIENTS:
- 418 grams of Canned pink Alaska salmon
- 350 grams Packet filo pastry
- 3 tablespoons Walnut oil
- 15 grams Margarine
- 25 grams of Plain flour
- 2 tablespoons Greek yogurt
- 175 grams of Seafood sticks; chopped
- 25 grams Walnuts, chopped
- 100 grams Grated Parmesan OR- grated Cheddar cheese

INSTRUCTIONS:
a) Pre-heat oven to 80 C, 350 F, Gas mark 4. Lightly grease 8 individual pie dishes or ovenproof pudding bowls.
b) Drain the can of salmon and make the juice up to 200ml / 7fl.ounces with water for fish stock. Flake the salmon. Set aside.
c) Brush each sheet of filo pastry with oil and fold into sixteen 12.5cm / 5inch squares. Put one square into each pie dish leaving the pointed corners protruding over the edge.
d) Brush with oil then put a second square of the pastry onto the first, but with the corners pointing up in between the original ones to create a water lily effect. Brush the points well with oil then bake for 5 minutes to set but not brown. Take it out of the oven.
e) Reduce the oven temperature to 150 C, 300 F, Gas mark 2. Melt the margarine and stir in the flour. Blend in the fish stock, beating well to remove lumps. Stir the yogurt, seafood sticks, walnuts, and flaked salmon into the sauce and divide equally between the 8 pastry cases.
f) Sprinkle the breadcrumbs over the top then return to the oven to heat through for 5-8 minutes or until the cheese and pastry have turned golden brown. Serve immediately.

35. Crawfish and spicy cheese tart

Makes: 6 Servings

INGREDIENTS:
- 1 homemade or prepared basic pie dough, chilled
- 3 tablespoon butter
- ¼ cup diced red pepper
- ½ cup diced onions
- 3 tablespoon flour
- 1 pound crawfish tails
- 1 cup grated hot pepper Monterey jack cheese
- 2 tablespoons chopped green onions
- 1 salt; to taste
- 1 cayenne pepper; to taste

INSTRUCTIONS:
a) Preheat oven to 350 degrees. On a floured surface roll out the dough to a 10-inch circle. Transfer to a large lightly-greased cookie sheet.
b) In a sauté pan melt butter. When it begins to foam add red peppers and onions, and cook for 2 minutes. Add flour and cook, stirring, for 3 minutes. Add crawfish and cook for 2 minutes more. Remove from heat and fold in cheese and green onions.
c) Season to taste with salt and cayenne. Mound crawfish mixture in the center of the pastry circle, leaving a 2- to 3-inch border of the pastry. Fold excess pastry up over the filling, layering it over, but not completely covering the filling. Work around the circle, continuing to fold over the previous fold, until it forms a rustic, free-form tart.
d) Slide the cookie sheet into the oven and bake for 35 minutes.

36. Scallops and blue cheese tart

Makes: 1 serving

INGREDIENTS:
- 6 large Scallops
- 8 Red onions
- 6 oz Blue cheese
- 2 oz Mascarpone cheese
- 1 Egg yolk
- 4 oz Spinach leaves
- Vinegar
- Sugar
- Red wine
- Parsley

INSTRUCTIONS:
a) To make this dish you need to cook the onions first.
b) To do this thinly slice them and cook them in a little olive oil. Slowly cook them for about 30 minutes with the vinegar.
c) Roll out the pastry and line a greased tin with the thin pastry before making the filling. Make the filling by mixing the mascarpone and blue cheese with the egg yolk and seasoning.
d) Blind bake the pastry in a hot oven. Remove and fill with the mixture and the sliced scallops. Bake in the oven and remove from the tin. Serve with the onion jam on the side.

37. Creamy smoked salmon and dill tart

Makes: 6 Servings

INGREDIENTS:
- 5 Sheet phyllo - thawed
- 3 tablespoons Unsalted butter - melted
- 4 large Egg yolks
- 1 tablespoon Dijon mustard - PLUS 1 teaspoon
- 3 large Eggs
- 1 cup Half and half
- 1 cup Whipping cream
- 6 ounces Smoked salmon - chopped
- 4 Green onions - chopped
- ¼ cup Dill - fresh, chopped OR 1 T. dried dill weed
- Dill sprigs

INSTRUCTIONS:
a) Generously butter a 9½-inch diameter deep-dish pie plate.
b) Place 1 phyllo sheet on the work surface.
c) Brush the phyllo sheet with butter and fold it in half lengthwise. Brush folded surface with butter.
d) Cut in half crosswise. Place 1 phyllo rectangle, buttered side down, in the prepared pie plate, covering the bottom and letting pastry overhang 1 section of edge by ½-inch.
e) Brush the top of the phyllo on a pie plate with butter. Place the second phyllo rectangle on a pie plate, covering the bottom and letting the pastry overhang another section of the edge by ½-inch; brush with butter.
f) Repeat the process with the remaining 4 phyllo sheets, making certain the entire surface of the edge is covered to form the crust.
g) Fold the overhang under to form a crust edge flush with the edge of the pie plate.
h) Brush crust edges with butter.
i) Preheat oven to 350F. Whisk yolks and mustard in a bowl to blend.

j) Beat in eggs, half and half, cream, salmon, onions, and chopped dill.
k) Season to taste with salt and pepper. Pour into prepared crust.
l) Bake until the center is set, about 50 minutes.
m) Transfer to rack. Cool. Garnish with dill sprigs and serve slightly warm or at room temperature.

38. Norwegian salmon tarts

Makes: 12 Servings

INGREDIENTS:
- 10 tablespoons Butter
- 2 cups Flour
- Water; cold
- 1 tablespoon Butter
- 1 large Onion; chopped
- 1 cup Mushrooms; sliced
- ½ cup Sour cream
- 1 pound Salmon fillet
- 2 Eggs; lightly beaten
- 2 teaspoons Dill; fresh, chopped
- Salt
- Pepper
- 1 Egg white; slightly beaten
- 1 cup Sour cream
- 2 teaspoons Chives; chopped
- 1 teaspoon Dill; fresh, chopped
- 1 dash of Garlic powder

INSTRUCTIONS:
a) Cut Butter into the flour with a pastry blender and add water, a little at a time, until a stiff dough is formed.
b) Roll and cut out the top and bottom crusts for 12 tarts.
c) In a skillet, melt butter, add onion, and brown.
d) Add mushrooms and sour cream; simmer for five minutes and cool.
e) Meanwhile, poach or steam fish until it flakes easily. Drain fish and flake in a bowl.
f) Mix whole eggs and dill with fish.
g) Season with salt and pepper to taste.
h) Blend the fish and the mushroom mixtures and spoon them into the bottom crusts. Top with the second crust and pinch the edges together to seal.

i) Brush egg white over the top crusts and edges.
j) Prick crusts for steam vents. Bake for 10 minutes at 450 degrees F., or until the crust is golden brown.
k) Mix sour cream and seasonings. Add a spoonful to each tart before serving.

39. Tiny smoked salmon tarts

Makes: 6 Servings

INGREDIENTS:
- 1¾ cup All-purpose flour
- ¼ teaspoon Salt John Culbertson Winery.
- 8 tablespoons Butter
- ¼ cup Cold water

INSTRUCTIONS:
a) Place the flour, salt, and butter in the bowl of a food processor.
b) Process until the dough resembles a meal.
c) Add water and process until the dough forms a ball on the blade.
d) Roll the dough out ¼-inch thick and cut it into 2-inch rounds. Line miniature tart pans with the dough rounds.
e) Filling: 4 ounces smoked salmon 5 ounces Gruyere cheese, shredded finely 4 each egg, beaten 1½ cups milk ½ cup whipping cream ¼ teaspoon salt ¼ teaspoon pepper
f) Blot the smoked salmon slices with a paper towel to remove excess moisture and then cut the slices into 1-inch slivers.
g) Divide the slivered salmon among the tart shells and sprinkle the cheese over each.
h) Mix the eggs, milk, and cream with the salt and pepper and pour into each tart shell.
i) Bake the tarts in a preheated 400 degrees F oven for about 15 minutes.
j) Keep checking during baking since the tarts are small and take much less time than would a larger tart.

40. Festive shrimp tarts

Makes: 48 servings

INGREDIENTS:
- 2 pastries for double-crust pie or tart shells.
- 1 cup Milk
- 1 pack of Cream cheese, cubed
- 4 Eggs, slightly beaten
- 1 can Baby shrimp, drained, or Fresh.
- 2 tablespoons Dried chives
- ¼ cup Finely chopped red pepper
- Salt and pepper to taste
- Fresh dill weed to garnish

INSTRUCTIONS:
a) Prepare 48 small tart shells from the pastry. Heat milk over low heat; add cream cheese cubes stirring until smoothly melted.
b) Gradually add cheese mixture to eggs; stir in remaining ingredients except for dill weed. Spoon 1 tablespoon of filling into each tart shell.
c) Bake at 350 F for 20-25 minutes or just until set. Garnish with reserved shrimp and dill weed. Makes: 48 small or 24 medium tarts.
d) Garnish before serving.

41. Shrimp, onion, and tomato tart

Makes: 1 serving

INGREDIENTS:
- 18 large Shrimp
- 10 Garlic cloves crushed
- 1 pinch Saffron
- 1 cup Olive oil
- 6 Onions
- 8-ounce can of Peeled tomatoes
- 2 Anchovies
- ¼ cup Kalamata olives
- 4 Sprigs thyme
- 1 Sheet puff pastry
- 2 Heads frisée
- 6 bunches Mache

INSTRUCTIONS:
a) A day in advance of preparing this dish, marinate shrimp in a mixture of 4 cloves crushed garlic, black pepper, ½ cup olive oil, and 1 pinch of saffron. Refrigerate overnight.
b) To prepare the marmalade, peel onions and cut them in half, and slice thin.
c) In a saucepan over low heat with 2 tablespoons of oil, cook the onions until transparent.
d) Drain the tomatoes, remove the seeds, chop roughly, and add to the onions.
e) Add chopped anchovies, chopped olives, and thyme, and cook for 3 hours on very low heat, stirring often.
f) Meanwhile, cut out 6 rounds of puff pastry about 3½ inches in diameter.
g) Place on a baking sheet cover with a second sheet, and bake in the oven for 6 minutes at 350 degrees.
h) Prepare the frisée by cutting off the green of the lettuce, using only the white part only. Chop frisée and wash well reserve.

i) In a large sauté pan over medium-high heat, heat ¼ cup olive until hot, and cook shrimp until pink and curled.

j) Set the tomato marmalade on top of each tart round and warm in the oven for 5 minutes. Season the frisée with a little olive oil, salt, and pepper.

k) Take the tart out of the oven and set it on a plate, dress some frisée on top of the tart, and cover it with shrimp.

l) Garnish with the Mache lettuce leaves.

m)   Drizzle olive oil around the tart and serve.

42. Shrimp cocktail tarts

Makes: 20 Appetizers

INGREDIENTS:
- 1 15 ounces pkg. refrigerated pie crusts
- Finely chopped leaf lettuce
- 1 12 ounces pkg. frozen small cooked shrimp, thawed, rinsed, drained
- Cocktail sauce

INSTRUCTIONS:
a) Heat oven to 450F. Allow both pie crust pouches to stand at room temperature for 15 to 20 minutes.
b) Unfold each crust; remove the top plastic sheet.
c) Press out fold lines. Invert and remove the remaining plastic sheet. Cut about ten 3-inch circles from each crust.
d) Fit circles over the backs of miniature muffin cups.
e) Pinch 4 or 5 equally spaced pleats around the sides of the cup.
f) Prick generously with a fork. Bake at 450F for 9 to 13 minutes or until light golden brown. Cool completely; remove from muffin cups.
g) Place a small amount of chopped lettuce in each tart shell. Spoon shrimp pieces over the lettuce layer.
h) Top with a small amount of cocktail sauce.

NUT TARTS

43. Almond tart

Makes: 8 servings

INGREDIENTS:
- Pastry
- ½ cup Heavy cream
- ⅓ cup Sugar
- 1 teaspoon Grated orange rind
- ¼ teaspoon Almond extract
- 1 cup Sliced almonds
- Whipped cream for garnish
- Raspberry preserves

INSTRUCTIONS:
a) At least 2 flours before preparing tart, make Pastry.
b) When the pastry has chilled, heat oven to 375'F. Between floured sheets of waxed paper, roll out the pastry to an 11-inch round. Fit into a 9-inch fluted tart pan with removable bottom.
c) Trim the pastry even with the edge of the pan.
d) Pierce the bottom and sides of the pastry.
e) Place the tart pan on the rimmed baking sheet. Line the pastry shell with aluminum foil and fill it with pie weights. Bake for 8 minutes; remove the pan from the oven and lift out the foil and weights. Return pastry to oven and bake 4 minutes longer. Set aside on a wire rack to cool.
f) Meanwhile, in a bowl, with an electric mixer on medium speed, stir together cream, sugar, rind, and extract until sugar has dissolved, Fold in almonds.
g) Spoon the almond mixture evenly into the pastry shell. Return to oven and bake 20 to 25 minutes, or until filling is golden. Cool to room temperature on a wire rack.
h) When the tart is cool, if desired, spoon whipped cream around the outer edge; stir preserves and drizzle over cream. Cut into 12 wedges and serve.
i) Pastry: In a bowl, combine 1 C unsifted all-purpose flour, ½ t salt, and ½ t sugar. With a pastry blender or 2 knives, cut in 6 T

unsalted butter and 2 T vegetable shortening until the mixture resembles coarse crumbs.

j) Gradually add 2½ to 3 T ice water to the flour mixture, mixing lightly with a fork until the pastry is moist enough to form a ball. With hands, roll into a ball and flatten to 1-inch thickness. Wrap and refrigerate at least 2 flours before using.

44. Mexican Chocolate Tart with Spiced Pecans

INGREDIENTS:
PECANS
- Nonstick vegetable oil spray
- 1 large egg white
- 2 tablespoons sugar
- 1 tablespoon golden brown sugar
- 1 teaspoon ground cinnamon
- ¼ teaspoon salt
- ⅛ teaspoon cayenne pepper
- 1 ½ cups pecan halves

CRUST
- 1 cup chocolate wafer cookie crumbs, finely ground in processor
- ¼ cup sugar
- ½ teaspoon ground cinnamon
- ⅛ teaspoon salt
- 5 tablespoons unsalted butter, melted

FILLING
- 1 cup heavy whipping cream
- 4 ounces bittersweet or semisweet chocolate, chopped
- A 3.1-ounce disk of Mexican chocolate
- ¼ cup unsalted butter, cut into 4 pieces
- 2 teaspoons vanilla extract
- 1 teaspoon ground cinnamon
- ¼ teaspoon salt
- Lightly sweetened whipped cream

INSTRUCTIONS:
FOR PECANS:
a) Preheat oven to 350°F. Spray rimmed baking sheet with nonstick spray.
b) Whisk all ingredients except pecans in a bowl. Stir in pecans.
c) Spread in a single layer on a sheet, rounded side up.
d) Bake until just browned and dry, about 30 minutes. Cool on sheet.

e) Separate nuts, removing the excess coating.

FOR CRUST:

f) Preheat oven to 350°F. Blend the first 4 ingredients in the processor.

g) Add melted butter; process until crumbs are moistened.

h) Press crumbs into a 9-inch-diameter tart pan with removable bottom, to within ⅛ inch of the top.

i) Bake until set, about 20 minutes. Cool on rack.

FOR FILLING:

j) Bring cream to a simmer in a medium saucepan. Remove from heat.

k) Add chocolates; whisk until melted. Add butter, 1 piece at a time; whisk until smooth.

l) Whisk in vanilla, cinnamon, and salt. Pour filling into the crust. Chill until the filling begins to set, about 15 to 20 minutes.

m) Arrange nuts in concentric circles atop the tart. Chill until set, about 4 hours.

45. Frangipane Tart with seasonal Fruit

INGREDIENTS:
- 1 serving pâte brisée
- 6 tablespoons unsalted butter, softened
- ½ cup sugar
- 1 large egg
- ¾ cup blanched almonds, ground fine
- 1 teaspoon almond extract
- 1 tablespoon Amaretto
- 1 tablespoon all-purpose flour
- 2 cups strawberries, hulled
- 2 cups raspberries, picked over and rinsed
- ¼ cup strawberry or raspberry jam, melted and strained

PÂTE BRISÉE
- 1¼ cups all-purpose flour
- 6 tablespoons cold unsalted butter, cut into bits 2 tablespoons cold vegetable shortening
- ¼ teaspoon salt

INSTRUCTIONS:
PÂTE BRISÉE
a) In a bowl blend the flour, butter, vegetable shortening, and salt until the mixture resembles a meal.
b) Add 2 tablespoons of ice water, toss the mixture until the water is incorporated, add more ice water if necessary to form a dough, and form the dough into a ball.
c) Dust the dough with flour and chill it, wrapped in wax paper, for 1 hour.

TART
d) Roll out the dough ⅛- an inch thick on a lightly floured surface, fit it into an 11-by 8 -inch rectangular or 10-or 11-inch round tart pan with a removable fluted rim, and chill the shell while making the frangipane.
e) In a bowl cream together the butter and the sugar and beat in the egg, the almonds, the almond extract, the Amaretto, and the flour.

f) Spread the frangipane evenly on the bottom of the shell and bake the tart in the middle of a preheated 375°F. oven for 20 to 25 minutes, or until the shell is pale golden.
g) Let the tart cool. Cut the strawberries lengthwise into ⅛-inch-thick slices, arrange the slices, overlapping, decoratively with the raspberries in rows on the frangipane, and brush them gently with the jam.

46. Bakewell Tart

INGREDIENTS:
- 1 Great Unshrinkable Sweet Tart Shell, partially baked in a 9-inch removable bottom tart pan
- 1 cup coarsely chopped almonds, blanched if you can find them
- 1 ½ tablespoons all-purpose flour
- ⅔ cup sugar
- 9 tablespoons unsalted butter, at room temperature
- 1 large egg
- 1 large egg white
- ½ teaspoon almond extract
- 1 ½ teaspoons orange zest
- ⅓ cup raspberry jam
- Slivered or sliced almonds, for garnish

INSTRUCTIONS:
a) Finely grind almonds and flour in a processor. Mix in sugar, then butter, extract, and orange zest. Blend until smooth. Mix in egg and egg white. Transfer the filling to a bowl. Cover and chill for at least 3 hours.

b) Position the rack in the center of the oven and preheat to 350°F. Spread jam over the base of the tart shell. Dollop the almond filling all over, then spread it carefully with an offset spatula. If using slivered or sliced almonds as a garnish, sprinkle them over the top now. Bake tart until golden and a tester inserted into the center of the filling comes out clean, about 45 minutes. Cool tart in pan on rack.

c) To serve, push the pan bottom up, releasing the tart from the pan. Cut tart into wedges and sprinkle with powdered sugar, if desired.

d) Do ahead: Almond filling can be made 2 days ahead. Keep chilled. Whole tart can also be made half a day in advance. Let stand at room temperature

47. Apple nut lattice tart

Makes: 1 serving

INGREDIENTS:
- 15-ounce package of Refrigerated Pie Crusts
- 3 cups Thinly sliced peeled apples
- ½ cup Sugar
- 3 tablespoons Golden raisins
- 3 tablespoons Chopped walnuts or pecans
- ½ teaspoon Cinnamon
- ¼ teaspoon Grated lemon peel
- 2 teaspoons Lemon juice
- 1 Egg yolk; beaten
- 1 teaspoon Water
- ¼ cup Powdered sugar
- 1 teaspoon Lemon juice

INSTRUCTIONS:
a) Prepare pie crust according to package directions for two-crust pie using a 10-inch tart pan with removable bottom or a 9-inch pie pan.

b) Place 1 prepared crust in pan; press in bottom and up sides of the pan. Trim edges if necessary.

c) Heat oven to 400 F. Place cookie sheet in the oven to preheat. In a bowl, combine apples, sugar, raisins, walnuts, cinnamon, lemon peel, and 2 teaspoons of lemon juice; toss lightly to coat. Spoon into the crust-lined pan.

d) To make a lattice top, cut the second crust into ½-inch-wide strips. Arrange strips in lattice design over filling. Trim and seal edges. In a bowl, combine egg yolk and water; gently brush over the lattice.

e) Place tart on preheated cookie sheet. Bake at 400 F. for 40 to 60 minutes or until the apples are tender and the crust is golden brown. Cover the edge of the crust with strips of foil after 15 to 20 minutes of baking to prevent excessive browning. Cool 1 hour.

f) In a bowl, combine glaze ingredients, adding enough lemon juice for desired drizzling consistency. Drizzle over a slightly warm tart. Cool; remove the sides of the pan.

48. Apricot macadamia nut tart

Makes: 12 Servings

INGREDIENTS:
- 1½ cup Flour
- ⅔ cup Butter; softened
- ¼ cup Brown sugar; packed
- 2 tablespoons Cocoa
- 1 Egg
- 8 ounces Dried apricots
- 3½ ounce Macadamia nuts; coarsely chopped
- ⅓ cup Sugar
- ¼ cup Butter; melted
- ½ cup Light corn syrup
- ¼ teaspoon Salt
- 2 Eggs

CHOCOLATE-DIPPED APRICOTS
- ¼ cup Semisweet chocolate chips
- 1 teaspoon Shortening
- 12 Dried apricots

INSTRUCTIONS:
a) Heat oven to 400¼. Mix all pastry ingredients until dough forms.
b) Press firmly and evenly against the bottom and side of an ungreased 11-inch tart pan with removable bottom. Bake for 10-12 minutes or until set.
c) After baking the pastry, heat the oven to 375 ¼. Reserve 12 apricots for Chocolate-dipped Apricots; coarsely chop the remaining apricots.
d) Sprinkle nuts and chopped apricots evenly over the baked pastry.
e) Beat sugar, butter, corn syrup, salt, and eggs until smooth. Pour over nuts and apricots.
f) Bake for 25 to 30 minutes or until set.

g) Line the plate with waxed paper. Place chips and shortening in a small microwave-safe bowl. Microwave uncovered on medium for 2 to 3 minutes or until the mixture can be stirred smoothly.
h) Dip half of each apricot into the chocolate mixture; place on a plate.
i) Let stand until the chocolate is dry. Place on the tart.

49. Blackberry cream nut tart

Makes: 1 serving

INGREDIENTS:
- ⅓ cup All-purpose flour
- ½ teaspoon Salt
- 1 8-ounce package of cream cheese, softened
- ¼ cup Sweetened condensed milk
- 2 tablespoons Sifted powdered sugar
- 1 16-ounce package of frozen blackberries, thawed and drained
- ½ cup Granulated sugar
- 3 tablespoons Cornstarch
- ½ cup Finely ground walnuts
- 1½ cups Sifted powdered sugar
- 2 tablespoons Butter-flavored shortening
- ½ teaspoon Vanilla
- ½ cup Butter-flavored shortening
- 3 tablespoons Ice water
- 1 tablespoon Fresh lemon juice
- ¼ cup White chocolate chips
- ¼ cup Walnuts
- 2 tablespoons Boysenberry syrup
- 1 teaspoon Butter or margarine
- ½ teaspoon Fresh lemon juice
- ⅛ teaspoon Salt
- ½ teaspoon Butter flavoring
- 4 tablespoons whipping cream

INSTRUCTIONS:
a) To make the crust: Preheat oven to 425 degrees. Combine flour and salt in a bowl. Cut in shortening using a pastry blender or 2 knives until all flour is blended in to form pea-sized chunks.
b) Sprinkle with water, 1 tablespoon at a time. Toss lightly with a fork until the dough will form a ball. Press between hands to form a 5- to 6-inch "pancake."

c) Flour the rolling surface and rolling pin lightly. Roll the dough into a circle. Trim 1 inch larger than an upside-down 9-inch tart pan with removable sizes. Loosen the dough carefully. Fold into quarters. Flour tart pan lightly.

d) Unfold the dough and press it into the tart pan. Trim the edge even with the top of the rim. Prick the bottom and sides thoroughly with a fork 50 times to prevent shrinkage.

e) Cover the edge with a double layer of foil to prevent over-browning.

f) Bake for 10 to 15 minutes or until lightly browned. Cool to room temperature.

g) To make cream cheese filling: Combine cream cheese, condensed milk, powdered sugar, and lemon juice in a bowl. Beat at the low speed of an electric mixer until creamy. Place white chocolate chips and nuts in a food processor work bowl. Process until finely chopped. Blend into cheese mixture. Spread in the bottom of the cooled baked tart shell.

h) To make fruit filling: Combine blackberries, sugar, cornstarch, and boysenberry syrup in a medium saucepan. Cook and stir on medium heat until the mixture is thickened and clear. Remove from heat. Stir in butter, lemon juice, and salt. Transfer to a bowl. Cool to room temperature. Spoon over cheese filling.

i) To make topping: Sprinkle nuts over fruit filling in a lattice fashion.

j) To garnish: Combine powdered sugar, shortening, vanilla, butter flavoring, and 3 tablespoons of cream in a bowl. Beat until smooth, adding more cream, if needed, for desired consistency. Spoon into the decorator bag fitted with the desired tip. Form a decorative border around the edge of the tart.

k) Refrigerate for 1 to 2 hours. Remove rim. Cut into servings. Refrigerate leftovers.

50. Carrot-nut tart

Makes: 8 servings

INGREDIENTS:
- 1 Pie shell; partially baked
- 3 Eggs
- ⅓ cup Sugar
- 1 teaspoon Lemon juice and lemon zest
- 2 cups Finely shredded carrot
- 4 tablespoons Butter melted
- ½ teaspoon Baking powder
- ⅔ cup Flour
- ½ cup Almonds
- ¼ cup Apricot glaze

INSTRUCTIONS:

a) Mix eggs, sugar, lemon juice, and zest; add carrots and butter, and stir well.

b) In separate bowls mix nuts, flour, and baking powder. Blend two mixtures; pour into a partially baked pie or tart shell. Bake at 400 degrees for approximately 20 minutes.

c) For the glaze, meltdown apricot preserves, add 2 tablespoons of brandy and coat the top of the tart when the tart comes out of the oven.

51. Caramel-nut tart

Makes: 1 serving

INGREDIENTS:
- 1 cup Sugar
- ⅔ cup Heavy cream
- ¼ cup unsalted butter; cut into small pieces
- 3 tablespoons Honey
- ½ teaspoon Salt
- 2½ cups Walnut halves
- 1 serving of Pâte Sucrée dough
- 2 ounces Bittersweet chocolate; chopped
- 2½ cups All-purpose flour
- 3 tablespoons Sugar
- 2 Sticks cold unsalted butter; cut up
- 2 large Egg yolks
- 4 tablespoons Ice water

INSTRUCTIONS:
a) In a heavy saucepan, bring ¼ cup water and sugar to a boil, stirring until sugar is dissolved. Boil syrup in a covered pan, without stirring; you can either swirl the pan or wash down the sides of the pot with a pastry brush dipped in water to remove any sugar crystals that have clung until it begins to turn golden.

b) Carefully add cream and return the pan to heat. Add butter, honey, and salt, stirring until the butter has melted and the mixture is smooth. Stir in walnuts and simmer, uncovered, over medium heat, stirring occasionally, for about 5 minutes. Remove from heat and let cool.

c) Meanwhile, roll half of the pate Sucrée between 2 sheets of plastic wrap into an 11-inch circle. Fit pastry into a 9-inch fluted tart pan with a removable bottom. To trim the dough evenly, roll the rolling pin over the tart pan. Chill for 20 to 30 minutes.

d) Heat oven to 400. Fill the tart shell with a cooled walnut mixture, spreading evenly with a rubber spatula. Roll out the remaining dough between 2 sheets of plastic wrap into an 11-inch circle. Transfer to the tart shell. Press the top crust edge to the bottom crust to seal. Roll the rolling pin over the tart pan to trim the edge. Freeze for 20 minutes.

e) Bake on a parchment-lined baking sheet until the crust is golden, about 25 to 30 minutes. Cool on a wire rack.

f) In a double boiler over barely simmering water, melt chocolate, stirring until smooth. Cool chocolate and transfer to a pastry bag fitted with a very small plain tip.

g) Pipe chocolate in a circular pattern over the entire surface of the tart. Let chocolate set at room temperature, for about 1 to 2 hours.

PATE SUCRÉE

h) Place the flour and sugar in the food processor; pulse to combine.

i) Add butter; pulse until the mixture resembles coarse meal, 10 to 20 seconds.

j) Lightly beat egg yolks; add ice water. Add to the food processor while the machine is running; process until the dough holds together.

k) Divide dough into two batches; turn out into two separate pieces of plastic wrap.

l) Flatten each into a circle, and wrap in plastic wrap; refrigerate for at least 1 hour.

52. **Nut fruit tarts**

Makes: 6 Servings

INGREDIENTS:
- 1½ cup Whipping cream
- 1½ cups Puffed raisins
- 1 cup Chopped nuts
- ½ cup Sugar
- 2 Bananas, sliced
- 6 Maraschino cherries, chopped
- Few grains salt

INSTRUCTIONS:
a) Whip cream until stiff. Fold in sugar and salt. Divide into 2 portions.
b) Combine bananas and raisins with ½ the cream. Pile lightly in baked individual pastry shells. Cover with remaining cream. Garnish with cherries and nuts. 20 servings.

53. Orange brazil nut tart

Makes: 4 servings

INGREDIENTS:
- 3 Eggs, separated
- ¾ cup Granulated sugar
- Grated zest of 1 orange
- 1 teaspoon Vanilla extract
- 2 cups Finely ground Brazil nuts
- 1½ tablespoon All-purpose flour
- ¼ teaspoon Salt
- Garnish:
- 2 Grapefruits
- 2 Oranges
- 4 large Egg whites
- 1¼ cup Granulated sugar

INSTRUCTIONS:
a) Preheat the oven to 350 degrees. Line a 10-inch round cake pan with parchment paper, butter, and flour.
b) In a bowl, whip together the egg yolks and sugar until pale yellow. Add the orange zest and vanilla, whip until light and fluffy, and set aside.
c) In a bowl, combine 1 cup of Brazil nuts with the flour and set aside. Reserve the remaining nuts for the garnish.
d) In another bowl, beat the egg whites until foamy. Sprinkle in the salt and continue beating until soft peaks form. Alternate folding in the nut and flour mixture, and the beaten yolk mixture, until combined. Pour into the prepared pan.
e) Bake for 25 to 30 minutes, or until lightly browned. Set on a rack to cool, for about 10 minutes. Run a knife along the edge to loosen and invert onto a platter. Remove the parchment and let cool completely.
f) Meanwhile, preheat the oven to 300 degrees. Place the cake on a baking sheet lined with parchment paper.

g) Working over a bowl to catch the juices, peel the grapefruits and oranges and cut between the membranes to remove the sections. Remove the seeds. Arrange the sections over the cake. Pour the juice through a strainer and drizzle over the cake.

h) In a bowl, whisk the egg whites until foamy. Gradually add the sugar, whisking until stiff peaks form, about 10 minutes. Gently fold in the reserved 1 cup of ground Brazil nuts.

i) Spread the meringue evenly over the cake and bake for ½ hour. Cool on a rack and serve.

54. Pine nut tart

Makes: 4 servings

INGREDIENTS:
- 1 Puff pastry sheet
- 2 cups Pine nuts
- 2 tablespoons Honey
- 1 cup Sugar
- 3 Eggs
- 3 tablespoons Extra-virgin olive oil
- Zest of 1 lemon
- 2 tablespoons walnut liqueur

INSTRUCTIONS:
a) Preheat oven to 425 degrees. Place pastry tightly into the shell, crimping the edges with extra pastry to help maintain the edges. Cover the pastry with parchment, fill it with dried white beans, and place in the oven.
b) Cook for 8 to 10 minutes, remove parchment and beans, and cook until dry and light golden brown, about 8 to 10 more minutes. Remove and allow to cool.
c) In a bowl, stir together pine nuts, honey, sugar, eggs, olive oil, lemon zest, and liquor until smooth. Pour into cooled pastry shell and bake 20 minutes, or until quite firm and lightly browned on top.
d) Allow to cool to room temperature and serve.

FRUIT TARTS

55. Almond-apricot tarts

Makes: 18 servings

INGREDIENTS:
- ½ cup Butter
- 3 Ounces cream cheese
- ⅓ cup Butter
- ½ cup Sugar
- 1 each Egg
- ½ teaspoon Vanilla package softened
- 1 cup All-purpose flour
- ⅔ cup Coarsely ground toasted blanched almonds
- ⅓ cup Apricot preserves
- slice Almonds

INSTRUCTIONS:
a) DOUGH: Beat the ½ cup of butter and the cream cheese with an electric mixer for 30 seconds. Stir in the flour. Cover and chill for 1 hour.

b) FILLING: Beat the ⅓ cup of butter with an electric mixer for 30 seconds. Beat in the sugar, then the egg and vanilla.

c) Stir in the ground almonds. Press 1 tablespoon of the dough evenly into the bottom and up the sides of each of eighteen 2- to 2 ½-inch tart pans.

d) Spoon 1 teaspoon of the almond filling onto each tart.

e) Bake on a baking sheet for 20 to 25 minutes in a 350F oven. Cool the tarts in the pans for about 10 minutes. Meanwhile, heat and stir the apricot preserves over low heat until melted.

f) Remove the tarts from the pans and place them on wire racks. While the tarts are still warm, brush the filling with the melted preserves.

g) Garnish with sliced almonds, if desired. Cool. Makes: 18 tarts.

56. Alsatian plum tart

Makes: 6 to 8

INGREDIENTS:
- Butter
- 7 Large red plums, pitted, each cut into 8 wedges
- 4 tablespoons Sugar
- 1 Pate Sucrée Dough
- ½ teaspoon Ground cinnamon
- 1 Egg white, beaten to blend
- Vanilla ice cream

INSTRUCTIONS:
a) Preheat oven to 400F. Line baking sheet with foil; butter foil.
b) Place plums on the prepared sheet, spacing evenly. Sprinkle with 2 tablespoons of sugar. Bake until plums are tender but still hold shape, about 30 minutes. Cool plums on sheet.
c) Roll out dough on a floured surface to a 12-inch-diameter round.
d) Transfer the pastry to the center of another heavy large baking sheet. Overlap plums in concentric circles on the pastry, forming a 9-inch-diameter circle in the center.
e) Combine the remaining 2 tablespoons of sugar and cinnamon in a bowl. Sprinkle sugar mixture over plums. Fold the edge of the pastry over the plums, pinching to seal any cracks in the pastry. Brush the crust twice with egg white.
f) Bake tart until crust is golden, about 25 minutes. Run a thin sharp knife carefully under tart edges to loosen the sheet. Cool for 15 to 30 minutes. Serve tart and slightly warm with ice cream.

57. Apple tart

Makes: 4 servings

INGREDIENTS:
SWEET PASTRY DOUGH:
- 1 cup Flour
- 3 tablespoons Sugar
- ¼ teaspoon Baking powder
- pinch Salt
- 4 tablespoons Unsalted butter
- 1 large Egg

APPLE FILLING:
- 3 Golden Delicious Apples
- 2 tablespoons Sugar
- ¼ teaspoon Cinnamon

KIRSCH CUSTARD:
- ⅔ cup Heavy cream
- 3 tablespoons Sugar
- 1 tablespoon Kirsch
- 3 Egg yolks

INSTRUCTIONS:
a) For the dough, combine dry ingredients in a food processor and pulse to mix. Add butter and pulse in. Add egg and continue to pulse until dough forms a ball. Roll the dough into a 14-inch disk and line a 10-inch tart pan. Chill the dough for several hours, or overnight.

b) Peel, core, halve and slice the apples ⅛-inch thick; arrange on pastry, overlapping. Sprinkle with cinnamon sugar. For the custard, combine all ingredients; whisk by hand until smooth and well blended; strain and reserve.

c) Bake at 350 degrees for about 35 minutes or until apples and crust are baked through. Remove tart from oven; pour on custard cream, being careful not to let it overflow. Return the tart to the oven for 5 to 10 minutes or until the custard is set, but not colored or puffed.

58. Apple and raisin tarte tatin

Makes: 6 Servings

INGREDIENTS:
- 2 tablespoons Butter
- 3 tablespoons Rum
- 1 cup Mixed raisins and currants
- 2 pounds Med apples
- 17 ounces package of frozen puff pastry
- ¼ cup Plus 2 Tablespoons white sugar
- Oven: 400F

INSTRUCTIONS:
a) Peel, core, and cut apples into eighths. Fill a bowl, large enough to set a 9" cast iron fry pan in, with ice cubes, and then top up with water. Melt butter in a 9" cast iron fry pan over medium heat. Add sugar.

b) Stir until brown and JUST caramelized. Place fry pan in ice water to harden then onto a cooling rack. Set oven. Place raisins and currants in a bowl. Add rum and cover with hot water. Drain after 5 or so minutes.

c) Sprinkle a third of the raisins and currants over the caramel. Place apple slices, rounded side down and packed as close together as possible, in a circular pattern. Sprinkle with remaining raisins and currants.

d) Cut pastry 2 inches larger than a skillet. Put the pastry on top and tuck down the sides and under the edge of the outside row of apples. Bake for 30 minutes and then turn out onto a decorative plate while still hot.

e) Serve while still warm with freshly whipped cream.

59. Apple cinnamon tart

Makes: 10 servings

INGREDIENTS:
- 1½ cups Rolled oats
- 1 tablespoon Cinnamon
- ½ teaspoon Cinnamon
- ¾ cup Apple juice
- 2 large Apples, peeled/slices
- 1 teaspoon Lemon juice
- ⅓ cup cold Water
- 1 pack of Unflavored gelatin
- 2 cups Fat-free yogurt
- ¼ cup Honey
- ½ teaspoon Almond extract

INSTRUCTIONS:
a) Preheat oven to 350. Prepare a pie plate with cooking spray. In a bowl, combine oats and 1 tablespoon of cinnamon.
b) Toss with ¼ cup apple juice. Press onto the bottom of the pie plate. Bake for 5 minutes or until set. Cool. In a bowl, toss apple slices with lemon juice; arrange on cooled crust in pan and set aside.
c) In a pan, combine water and the remaining ½ cup of apple juice. Sprinkle gelatin over the water mixture; let stand for 3 minutes to soften.
d) Cook and stir over medium heat until gelatin is completely dissolved; remove from heat. Add yogurt, honey, remaining ½ teaspoon cinnamon, and almond extract; blend well.
e) Pour over apples in the crust. Chill for several hours or overnight.

60. Apple cranberry upside-down tart

Makes:1

INGREDIENTS:
- ⅔ cup Sugar
- 3 tablespoons Water
- 6 Tart apples, peeled, cored, and thinly sliced
- 1 cup Cranberries
- 3 tablespoons Sugar
- 1 tablespoon Butter
- 1 Unbaked pie shell

INSTRUCTIONS:
a) Simmer ⅔ cup sugar and 3 Tablespoons water in a small covered saucepan for 5 minutes. Uncover and boil until a golden thick caramel.
b) Remove immediately from heat so the caramel doesn't burn. Pour into a 10-inch glass or metal pie plate. Swirl to coat bottom.
c) Overlap one-third of the apple slices on the caramel.
d) Top with one-third of the cranberries and sprinkle with 1 tablespoon of sugar. Repeat twice with remaining fruit and sugar, Dot with butter.
e) Lay pastry loosely over fruit. Bake at 400 for 30 minutes. Remove to a rack and cool for 5 minutes. Tilt the pie plate over the bowl and pour off any accumulated juices. Invert the serving plate over the pie. Turn both over together.
f) Lift off the pie plate. Serve tart warm with vanilla ice cream.

61. Apple raspberry tart

Makes: 8 servings

INGREDIENTS:
- 1 cup All-purpose flour
- ½ teaspoon Salt
- ⅓ cup Shortening
- 2 tablespoons Cold water; up to 3
- 1 Egg; separated
- 23 ounces of Chunky Apple Sauce
- 1 cup Fresh raspberries OR 10 ounces pkg. frozen; thawed, drained
- 2 tablespoons Sugar
- ½ teaspoon Cinnamon
- ¾ cup All-purpose flour
- ½ cup Firmly packed brown sugar
- ½ teaspoon Cinnamon
- ⅓ cup Margarine or butter; softened

INSTRUCTIONS:
a) Heat oven to 400F.
b) In a bowl, combine flour and salt. Using a pastry blender or 2 knives, cut shortening into the flour mixture until particles are the size of small peas.
c) Gradually add water, tossing with a fork until the mixture is moistened.
d) Gather pastry into a ball. Flatten ball. Roll out on a lightly floured surface from the center to edge into a circle 1½ inches larger than the inverted 9-inch tart pan.
e) Fold dough in half; place in pan. Unfold; press in the bottom and up sides of the pan. Trim edges if necessary.
f) Bake at 400F for 5 minutes. Remove from oven; reduce oven temperature to 375F. In a bowl, beat egg white. Brush over the entire surface of the partially baked crust. Reserve the yolk for filling.

g) In a bowl, combine apple sauce, raspberries, sugar, ½ teaspoon cinnamon, and egg yolk. Pour into pastry-lined pan.

h) In a bowl, combine all topping ingredients; sprinkle over the fruit mixture. Bake at 375F for 40 to 50 minutes or until the topping is golden brown.

i) Cool; remove the sides of the pan. Serve with whipped cream.

62. Blueberry buttermilk tart

Makes: 1 serving

INGREDIENTS:
SHELL
- 1½ cups All-purpose flour
- ¼ cup Sugar
- ¼ teaspoon Salt
- ¼ pounds Cold butter; cut bits
- 1 large Egg; beat with
- 2 tablespoons Ice water
- Raw rice; for weighing shell

BUTTERMILK FILLING
- 1 cup Buttermilk
- 3 large Egg yolks
- ½ cup Sugar
- 1 tablespoon Lemon zest; grate
- 1 tablespoon Fresh lemon juice
- ½ Stick unsalted butter; melt, cool
- 1 teaspoon Vanilla
- ½ teaspoon Salt
- 2 tablespoons All-purpose flour
- 2 cups Blueberries; pick over
- Confectioner's sugar

INSTRUCTIONS:
SHELL
a) In a bowl, stir together flour, sugar, and salt. Add butter and blend until the mixture resembles a coarse meal. Add yolk mixture, toss until liquid is incorporated, and form dough into a disk. Dust dough with flour and chill, wrapped in plastic wrap, for 1 hour. Roll out dough ⅛" thick on a floured surface and fit into a 10" tart pan with a removable fluted rim.
b) Chill shell for at least 30 minutes or, covered, overnight.
c) Preheat oven to 350 degrees.

d) Line the shell with foil and fill it with rice. Bake the shell in the middle of the oven for 25 minutes.

e) Remove foil and rice carefully and Bake the shell 5 minutes more, or until pale golden. Cool shell in pan on a rack.

FILLING

f) In a blender or processor blend the filling ingredients until smooth. Spread blueberries evenly in the bottom of the shell.

g) Pour buttermilk filling over blueberries and bake in the middle of the oven for 30 to 35 minutes or until just set.

h) Remove the rim of the pan and cool the tart completely in the pan on the rack. Sift confectioners' sugar over the tart and serve at room temp or chilled with blueberry ice cream. Source: Conde Nast's Gourmet's Weekends.

63. Mixed fruit tart

Makes: 8 servings

INGREDIENTS:
- ¼ cup Raisins
- ½ cup Boiling water
- 8 slices white bread
- 1½ cups 1% Low-fat milk, divided
- 1 cup Peeled, chopped pear
- 2 tablespoons Flour
- ¼ cup + 2 Tb. sugar, divided
- 2 tablespoons Cornmeal
- 1 teaspoon Grated lemon rind
- 3 Eggs, lightly beaten
- ½ cup Seedless red grapes halved
- 2 teaspoons Chopped fresh rosemary
- 2 teaspoons Olive oil

INSTRUCTIONS:
a) Combine raisins and boiling water; let stand for 15 minutes. Drain and set aside.
b) Trim crusts from bread. Cut each slice into 4 triangles; place in a single layer in a 13 x 9 x 3 baking dish. Pour ½ cup milk over the bread and let stand for 5 minutes.
c) Carefully arrange the bread triangles in the bottom of a 10" quiche dish coated with cooking spray.
d) Top with apple and pear.
e) Place flour in a bowl, and gradually add remaining milk stirring with a wire whisk until blended.
f) Stir in sugar, cornmeal, lemon rind, and eggs; stir well.
g) Pour milk mixture over apple and pear; top with raisins and grapes, and sprinkle with rosemary.
h) Drizzle oil over the mixture; sprinkle with remaining sugar.
i) Bake at 350F for 50 minutes or until set; cool on a wire rack. Cut into wedges.

64. **Holiday fruit tarts**

Makes: 10 servings

INGREDIENTS:
- 3 cups Plain nonfat yogurt
- Cooking Spray
- 1¾ cup Regular oats, uncooked
- ¼ cup Firmly packed brown sugar
- 2 tablespoons All-purpose flour
- ½ cup Raspberry Spreadable Fruit
- 6 tablespoons Margarine, melted
- 12 ounces of Low-fat cream cheese, softened
- 6 tablespoons Sugar
- 1½ tablespoon Grated lemon rind
- 1½ tablespoon Lemon juice
- 2 cups Frozen raspberries, thawed and drained

INSTRUCTIONS:
a) Place yogurt in a coffee filter-lined colander; set it over a bowl and cover it with plastic wrap. Refrigerate and drain for 12 hours.
b) Preheat oven to 350'F.; spray ten 4½" tartlet pans with PAM. In a food processor bowl process oats, brown sugar, and flour until finely ground.
c) Add margarine; process until combined. Place 3 tablespoons oat mixture in each tartlet pan; press evenly on the bottom and ½" up sides. Place tartlet pans on a jelly roll sheet; bake for 15-17 minutes or until golden. Cool completely on wire racks.
d) In a bowl, beat cream cheese until smooth. Stir in drained yogurt, sugar, lemon rind, and juice. Spoon evenly into prepared crusts. Top with 2 tablespoons of fruit sauce, cover, and chill for at least 3 hours.
e) FRUIT SAUCE: In a medium saucepan stir All Fruit over low heat until smooth; stir in fruit.

65. Rainbow fruit tart

Makes: 8 servings

INGREDIENTS:
- ½ Serving of Sweet Dough for Pies and Tarts

WHITE CHOCOLATE FILLING
- ⅔ cup Heavy cream
- 10 ounces White chocolate
- 1 tablespoon Kirsch or white rum

FINISHING
- 1 pint Strawberries
- 2 Kiwis
- ½ pint Raspberries
- Toasted sliced almonds or chopped
- Pistachios
- Confectioners' sugar

INSTRUCTIONS:
a) For the tart crust, preheat the oven to 350 degrees and set a rack in the middle level. Butter the tart pan. On a floured surface, roll the dough and line a 9-inch tart pan with it. Pierce the dough all over with the tines of a fork and line it with a piece of parchment or waxed paper.
b) Fill with dry beans. Bake the tart shell for about 20 to 30 minutes, until it is dry and a deep golden color. Cool the tart shell on a rack.
c) For the chocolate filling, bring the cream to a boil in a medium saucepan over low heat.
d) Remove from heat and add chocolate all at once. Shake the pan so that all the chocolate is submerged and let stand for 3 minutes to melt the chocolate.
e) Add liqueur and whisk smooth. Pour the filling into a bowl and refrigerate it until thickened, but not hardened, about 20 minutes, stirring occasionally while it is chilling.
f) Whisk the filling slightly to make it smooth enough to spread.
g) Spread the filling evenly in the cooled tart shell.

h) Arrange the fruit in concentric rows on the chocolate filling, pressing them in slightly.

i) To unmold the tart, stand the tart pan on a large can or canister and allow the pan side to fall away.

j) Slide tart from the pan bottom to a large, flat-bottomed platter.

k) Immediately before serving, edge the tart with the almonds or pistachios and dust with the confectioners' sugar.

66. Vanilla cream fruit tart

Makes: 12 Servings

INGREDIENTS:
- ¾ cup Butter or margarine --Softened
- ½ cup Confectioner's sugar
- 1½ cups All-purpose flour
- 10 ounces Package of vanilla chips, melted and cooled
- ¼ cup Whipping cream
- 8 ounces Package of cream cheese, softened
- 1 pint of Fresh strawberries, Sliced
- 1 cup Fresh blueberries
- 1 cup Fresh raspberries
- ½ cup Pineapple juice
- ¼ cup Sugar
- 1 tablespoon Cornstarch
- ½ teaspoon Lemon juice

INSTRUCTIONS:
a) In a bowl, cream butter and confectioner's sugar. Beat in flour.
b) Pat into the bottom of a greased 12-inch pizza pan.
c) Bake at 300 for 25-28 minutes or until lightly browned.
d) Cool. In another bowl, beat melted chips and cream.
e) Add cream cheese; beat until smooth. Spread over crust. Chill for 30 minutes.
f) Arrange berries over filling. In a saucepan, combine pineapple juice, sugar, cornstarch, and lemon juice; bring to a boil over medium heat.
g) Boil for 2 minutes or until thickened, stirring constantly.
h) Cool; brush over fruit. Chill 1 hour before serving. Store in the refrigerator.

67. Parisienne fruit tart

Makes: 6 Servings

INGREDIENTS:
- 10 ounces package of frozen patty shells
- Sugar
- 1 cup Milk
- 1 cup Heavy cream
- 4 ounces package of vanilla-flavor soft dessert mix
- 2 bananas
- 2 tablespoons Lemon juice
- ⅓ cup Apricot preserves
- 2 cups Seedless green grapes, washed
- 8¼ ounces sliced pineapple, drained.

INSTRUCTIONS:
a) Remove patty shells from the package. Thaw at room temperature for one-half hour.
b) Place rounds of the pastry, overlapping slightly, lengthwise on a lightly floured surface. Roll to a 16x4 inch rectangle.
c) Place on an ungreased large cookie sheet; trim edges evenly; prick well with a fork; chill for 30 minutes.
d) Reroll trimmings thinly; cut into ⅓-inch wide strips about 4 inches long; brush with water; press ends together to make rings.
e) Brush rings with water, then dip in sugar; place on the cookie sheet along with the rectangle of the pastry.
f) Bake pastry and pastry ring in the oven at 400 degrees for 10 minutes. reserve rings for decoration.
g) Bake pastry rectangle 10 minutes longer, or until golden brown.
h) Remove to wire rack; cool.
i) Combine milk, ¼ cup of the cream, and dessert mix in a small deep bowl; beat, following label instructions. Chill for 15 minutes.
j) Peel and cut bananas into ¼-inch thick slices. Sprinkle with half the lemon juice.
k) Split the pastry into two layers.

l) Place the bottom layer on a long serving dish or board; spread with about ⅔ of the soft dessert; arrange banana slices on long side edges; spread with remaining dessert mix.
m) Top with a second pastry layer.
n) Heat apricot preserves with remaining lemon juice until melted in a pan; cool slightly. Brush all over the tart.
o) Beat remaining cream until stiff in a bowl.
p) Pope or spread whipped cream over top of the pastry.
q) Arrange neat rows of grapes in cream, starting at the outer edges.
r) Cut pineapple slices in half and place in the center.
s) Garnish with reserved pastry rings.

68. Premier white fruit tart

Makes: 1 serving

INGREDIENTS:
- Pastry for single-crust; 9-inch pie
- ⅓ cup Granulated sugar
- ¼ cup All-purpose flour
- 3 Egg yolks
- 1 cup Milk
- 6 ounces package of White Baking Bars, chopped
- 1 teaspoon Vanilla extract
- ¼ cup Apricot jam; warmed
- 2 Kiwifruit; peeled and sliced
- 1 cup Raspberries
- Premier White Leaves, optional

INSTRUCTIONS:
a) Line 9-inch tart pan with pastry; trim edges.
b) Prick the pastry with a fork. Bake in preheated 425-degree F. oven for 10 to 12 minutes until the crust is lightly browned. Cool to room temperature.
c) Combine sugar and flour in a pan; stir in egg yolks and milk.
d) Cook over medium heat, stirring constantly until the mixture comes to a boil.
e) Reduce heat. Simmer, stirring constantly, for 3 minutes until the mixture is thickened and smooth. Remove from heat.
f) Add baking bars and vanilla; stir until smooth.
g) Press plastic wrap directly on the surface of the filling; chill completely.
h) Remove tart shell from pan. Brush jam over the bottom; let stand for 5 minutes.
i) Spread with filling. Arrange fruit on top. Chill. Garnish with Premier White Leaves, if desired.

VEGETABLE TART

69. Alpine potato tart

Makes: 10 servings

INGREDIENTS:
- 7 large Idaho potatoes
- 3 cups Swiss cheese, shredded
- 3 cups Heavy cream
- 3 teaspoons Garlic, chopped
- 1 tablespoon Salt
- 2 teaspoons Black pepper, fresh cracked
- 1 tablespoon Fresh thyme leaf, chopped
- 1 teaspoon Butter, softened
- Preheat the oven to 300 degrees F.

INSTRUCTIONS:
a) Peel the potatoes and cut them into slices about ⅛-inch thick. Set aside.
b) In a bowl, combine the potato slices, half of the shredded cheese, and the cream, garlic, salt, pepper, and thyme. Mix until well blended.
c) Grease a 9-inch square cake pan or casserole dish with the softened butter on the bottom and sides. Place potato mixture in the bottom of the pan, and press firmly as you add. When the mixture is all in the pan, make sure it is packed firmly. Top with the remaining half of the cheese.
d) Bake in the preheated oven until the top is golden brown, about 1½ hours. Remove the potatoes from the oven and let them rest for 15 minutes before slicing. Slice into 2- to 3-inch squares.

70. Artichoke tart

Makes: 8 servings

INGREDIENTS:
- 1 blind-baked pie crust in a 10 flute; d
- 1 tart pan
- 2 tablespoons olive oil
- 1-ounce pancetta; julienned
- ½ cup minced onion
- 2 tablespoons minced shallots
- 6-ounce julienned artichoke hearts
- 1 tablespoon minced garlic
- ¼ cup heavy cream
- 3 tablespoon chiffonade of fresh basil
- 1 juice of one lemon
- ½ cup grated Parmigiano-Reggiano cheese
- ½ cup grated asiago cheese
- 1 salt; to taste
- 1 freshly-ground black pepper; to taste
- 1 cup herbed tomato sauce; warm
- 1 tablespoon chiffonade basil
- 2 tablespoons grated parmesan cheese

INSTRUCTIONS:
a) Preheat the oven to 350 degrees.
b) In a sauté pan, heat the olive oil.
c) Sauté the pancetta for 1 minute.
d) Add the onions and shallots, and sauté for 2 to 3 minutes.
e) Add the hearts and garlic and continue sautéing for 2 minutes.
f) Add the cream. Season with salt and pepper. Stir in the basil and lemon juice.
g) Remove from the heat and cool. Spread the artichoke mixture on the bottom of the tart pan. Sprinkle the cheese over the mixture.

h) Bake for 15 to 20 minutes or until the cheeses have melted and are golden brown. Spoon a pool of the sauce into the center of the plate. Place a slice of the tart in the center of the sauce.
i) Garnish with grated cheese and basil.

71. **Pumpkin pie cheesecake Tart**

Makes: 1

INGREDIENTS:
THE CRUST
- ¾ cup Almond Flour
- ½ cup Flaxseed Meal
- ¼ cup Butter
- 1 teaspoon Pumpkin Pie Spice
- 25 drops Liquid Stevia

THE FILLING
a) 6 ounces of Vegan Cream Cheese
b) ⅓ cup Pumpkin Puree
c) 2 Tablespoons Sour Cream
d) ¼ cup Vegan Heavy Cream
e) 3 Tablespoons Butter
f) ¼ teaspoons Pumpkin Pie Spice
g) 25 drops Liquid Stevia

INSTRUCTIONS:
a) Combine all the crust's dry ingredients and stir thoroughly.
b) Mash together the dry ingredients with the butter and liquid stevia until a dough forms.
c) For your mini tart pans, roll the dough into little spheres.
d) Press the dough against the side of the tart pan until it reaches and goes up the sides.
e) Combine all the filling ingredients in a bowl.
f) Blend the filling ingredients using an immersion blender.
g) Once the filling ingredients are smooth, distribute them into the crust and chill.
h) Remove from the fridge, slice, and top with whipped cream if desired.

72. Roast vegetable tarts

Makes: 1 serving

INGREDIENTS:
- 450 grams Potatoes; peeled, grated,
- 1 large Parsnip; peeled and grated
- 50 grams of Plain flour
- Salt and freshly ground pepper
- 3 L5ml vegetable oil
- 2 Peppers; cored and roughly chopped
- 1 Courgette; cut into chunks
- 2 Cloves garlic; crushed
- 1 Red onion; cut into chunks
- 2 125 g potatoes; well-scrubbed
- 25 grams Vegetarian pecorino; flakes

INSTRUCTIONS:
a) Pre-heat the oven to 220øC/425øF/Gas Mark 7
b) Mix the grated potato, parsnip, and flour; season with the salt and pepper, then bind together with 2 x 15ml spoon / 2 tablespoons of oil.
c) Divide into 4 mounds on a well-greased baking sheet and shape into 10cm / 4-inch nests with the edges slightly raised. Cover with cling film and chill for 30 minutes.
d) Meanwhile mix the peppers, courgette, garlic, and onion. Cut the potatoes lengthways into equal wedges and add them to the other vegetables.
e) Toss the vegetables in the remaining oil with salt and pepper then roast in the oven for 20 minutes.
f) Turn the vegetables over. Uncover the tarts and place them in the oven on a separate sheet, continue cooking for a further 20 minutes.
g) Transfer tarts to serving dishes and spoon in roasted vegetables.
h) Top with flakes of pecorino cheese and serve immediately.

73. Roasted vegetable and goats cheese brioche tart

Makes: 8 servings

INGREDIENTS:
- ½ oz Fresh yeast
- 3 ½ ounces Warm water
- 8 oz Strong plain white flour
- 1 oz Sugar
- 2 eggs
- 4 oz Unsalted butter
- 1 small Aubergine
- 1 medium Courgette
- 2 tablespoons Olive oil
- 15 g pack of fresh thyme
- 2 Cloves garlic; thickly sliced
- 1 Red pepper
- 3 ½oz Goats cheese; sliced
- Salt and freshly ground black pepper

INSTRUCTIONS:
a) Preheat the oven to 400 F.
b) Mix the yeast with warm water, add 4 tablespoons of the plain flour, cover the bowl with cling film, and leave in a warm place for 10-15 minutes.
c) Place the remaining flour into a bowl.
d) Add the sugar, eggs, yeast mixture, and a pinch of salt. Beat well for 5 minutes.
e) Cover the bowl with cling film, and leave the dough in a warm place for 30 minutes or until the dough has doubled in size.
f) Slice the aubergine and courgette lengthwise.
g) Place these on a baking sheet and brush with olive oil. Sprinkle 1 clove of garlic and some thyme on top. Bake for 10 minutes.
h) Place the red pepper on a separate tray, brush with olive oil, and sprinkle with garlic and thyme. Bake in the oven for 20 minutes until soft. When cool remove the skin.

i) When the brioche dough has doubled in size return the bowl to the mixer and gradually beat in the softened butter. Re-cover the bowl with cling film and place the bowl in a warm place for a further 30 minutes.

j) When the brioche has doubled in size, approximately 30-40 minutes remove it from the bowl. Lightly flour the work surface and roll out the dough to ¾ inch thick and place the dough in the base of a non-stick tin.

k) Arrange the goat cheese and roasted vegetables on top of the dough leaving ¾ inch around the outer edge. Sprinkle with fresh thyme and season with salt and freshly ground black pepper.

l) Bake in the oven for 35 minutes until golden brown.

m) Remove from the tin and brush with the remaining olive oil.

74. Savory vegetable tart

Makes: 6 Servings

INGREDIENTS:
PASTRY CRUST
- 2 cups Unbleached white flour
- ⅓ cup Whole wheat flour
- ½ teaspoon Salt
- ½ cup Vegetable oil
- 4 tablespoons Skim or low-fat milk; as needed, up to 5
- 4 teaspoons Olive oil
- 2 large Onions; sliced
- ½ teaspoon Salt
- ¼ teaspoon Freshly ground black pepper
- 2 mediums Zucchini; thinly sliced
- 3 Plum tomatoes; thinly sliced

INSTRUCTIONS:
a) Preheat oven to 400 F. In a bowl, mix both flour and salt.
b) Gradually add oil, tossing the mixture with a fork until crumbly. Stirring with a fork, add enough milk until the mixture comes together in a ball. Shape into a small disc.
c) Roll out dough between two sheets of wax paper into a 12-inch round about ¼ inch thick.
d) Remove the top sheet of paper and invert the dough, without stretching, into a 9-inch round tart pan with removable bottom.
e) Carefully peel off the top piece of wax paper. Fit dough along the bottom and sides of the tart pan and trim the edges.
f) Loosely line the crust with foil, and fill it with dried beans or pie weights.
g) Bake for 15 minutes. Remove foil and beans and bake until golden brown, about 15 minutes more. Transfer to a wire rack and let cool. Reduce oven temperature to 375 F.
h) In a large skillet, heat oil over medium heat.
i) Add onions and cook, stirring occasionally, until golden brown, 15 to 20 minutes.

j) Transfer to crust and spread evenly. Season with some salt and pepper.

k) Add zucchini to skillet and cook until lightly golden, about 2 minutes per side.

l) Arrange zucchini and tomato slices in alternate circles on top of onions, sprinkling with remaining salt and pepper. Bake until tomatoes soften, about 25 minutes. Serve warm, or transfer to a wire rack to cool, then refrigerate until ready to serve.

75. Vegetable custard tart

Makes: 1 serving

INGREDIENTS:
- ¼ pounds Assorted wild and exotic mushrooms
- 5 slices Red onions
- 5 slices Eggplant
- 10 slices Zucchini
- 10 slices Yellow squash
- ¼ cup Olive oil
- Salt and freshly ground black pepper to taste
- 4 large Egg yolks
- 2 cups Heavy cream
- ½ cup Freshly grated Parmigiano-Reggiano cheese
- 1 tablespoon Chopped fresh parsley leaves
- 1 dash Worcestershire sauce
- 1 dash of Hot sauce
- ½ Basic Pie Dough; rolled out

INSTRUCTIONS:
a) Preheat the oven to 400 degrees.
b) Put the mushrooms and vegetables in a bowl, add the olive oil, and season with salt and pepper. Toss to coat.
c) Spread the vegetables evenly on a large baking sheet and roast until lightly golden, about 20 minutes.
d) Remove from the oven and let cool.
e) Reduce the oven temperature to 350 degrees.
f) In another bowl, combine the egg yolks and heavy cream and whisk well. Add the cheese, parsley, Worcestershire, and hot sauce, and season with salt and pepper.
g) Whisk to blend.
h) Line a 10-inch deep pie pan with the pie crust and crimp the edges.
i) Layer the eggplant, then the squash, zucchini, mushrooms, and onions in the bottom of the pan.
j) Pour the egg mixture evenly over the top.

k) Bake until the center sets and the top is golden, about 50 minutes.

l) Remove from the oven and let cool for 5 minutes before slicing to serve.

CHEESE TARTS

76. Alsatian cheese tart

Makes: 10 servings

INGREDIENTS:
- 4 cups Cake flour
- ⅝ cup Sugar
- 2½ Sticks sweet butter
- 1 Whole egg
- 16 ounces of Ricotta cheese
- ¾ cup Heavy cream
- 4 large Eggs, separated
- dash Fresh lemon juice
- pinch Fresh vanilla bean seeds OR
- 2 drops to 3 drops of vanilla extract
- 2 tablespoons Kirsch
- ¾ cup to 1 cup of sugar
- ½ teaspoon Ground cinnamon
- 1 teaspoon Vanilla extract
- Grated rind of ½ lemon

INSTRUCTIONS:
a) Mix all ingredients well, without overworking the dough. Allow dough to rest for 30 minutes before use.
b) Preheat oven to 375F. Roll out dough on a floured surface and line the bottom and sides of a 9-inch to 10-inch tart/pie pan with the dough.
c) Beat ricotta and cream together in a bowl; add egg yolks, sugar, cinnamon, vanilla, kirsch, and lemon rind. Mix thoroughly until very smooth.
d) Beat egg whites until stiff and gently fold them into the batter.
e) Pour the batter into the pastry-lined pan.
f) Bake for 40 to 45 minutes, or until slightly puffed and very brown. Cool tart completely, then chill for several hours before cutting.

77. Amaretto cheesecake tarts

Makes: 24 servings

INGREDIENTS:
- ⅓ cup Sunflower seeds or almonds ground fine
- 8 ounces of Cream cheese
- 1 Egg
- ⅓ cup Unsweetened shredded coconut
- 2 tablespoons Honey
- 2 tablespoons Amaretto liqueur

INSTRUCTIONS:
a) Line the cups of two muffin tins with paper liners.
b) Combine sunflower seeds and coconut.
c) Place 1 teaspoon of this mixture in each liner.
d) Press down with the back of a spoon to cover the bottoms.
e) Preheat oven to 325F.
f) To make the filling, cut the cream cheese into 8 blocks and blend with egg, honey, and Amaretto in a food processor, blender, or bowl till smooth and creamy.
g) Place a tablespoon of the filling in each tartlet cup and bake for 15 minutes

78. **Belgian cheese tart**

Makes: 8 servings

INGREDIENTS:
- Shortbread
- ½ pounds of Cream Cheese
- 3 tablespoons Confectioners' Sugar
- 1 teaspoon Lemon Juice
- 2 Eggs; Large
- ⅔ cup Heavy Cream

INSTRUCTIONS:
a) Preheat the oven to 350 degrees F. In a bowl, beat together the cheese, sugar, and lemon juice until the mixture is light and fluffy. Add the eggs, one at a time beating well after each addition. Beat until very smooth after the last addition.
b) Stir in the cream and pour the mixture into the prepared crust.
c) Brush the top of the tart with an egg and confectioners' sugar that has been beaten together.
d) Bake for 25 minutes or until set. Cool to room temperature and then chill before serving.

79. Bell pepper and cheese tart

Makes: 6 Servings

INGREDIENTS:
- 1½ cups All-purpose flour
- 1 teaspoon Sugar
- ¼ teaspoon Salt
- ½ cup chilled unsalted butter, cut into pieces
- 4 tablespoons ice water
- 10 Asparagus spears, trimmed, and cut into 1-inch pieces
- 3 tablespoons Olive oil
- 2 Red bell peppers, cut into matchstick-size strips
- 2 Green bell peppers, cut into matchstick-size strips
- 2 smalls Leeks, cut into matchstick-size strips
- 1 cup Grated Gruyere cheese
- 1 cup Grated mozzarella cheese

INSTRUCTIONS:
FOR CRUST:
a) Blend flour, sugar, and salt in a food processor.
b) Add butter and cut in using on/off turns until the mixture resembles a coarse meal.
c) Blend in enough water by the tablespoon until the dough begins to clump together.
d) Gather dough into a ball; flatten it into a disk.
e) Wrap in plastic and refrigerate for 1 hour.
f) Preheat oven to 350'F.
g) Grease a 9-inch-diameter tart pan with removable bottom.
h) Roll out dough on a lightly floured work surface to ⅛-inch-thick round. Transfer the dough to the prepared tart pan. Trim edges.
i) Freeze for 15 minutes. Line crust with foil. Fill with dried beans. Bake for 15 minutes.
j) Remove foil and beans.
k) Bake until lightly golden on the edges, about 15 minutes.

FOR FILLING:

l) Bring a large pot of water to a boil. Add asparagus and blanch for 2 minutes. Drain. Transfer to a bowl of ice water and cool.

m) Drain. Heat oil in a heavy large skillet over high heat. Add bell peppers and leeks and sauté until just tender, about 10 minutes.

n) Transfer to a bowl. Mix in asparagus.

o) Preheat oven to 350'F. Mix Gruyere into vegetables.

p) Transfer the mixture to the crust.

q) Sprinkle with mozzarella cheese. Bake tart until cheese melts, about 10 minutes. Serve hot.

80. Breakfast cheese tart

Makes: 1 serving

INGREDIENTS:
- Pastry for 9-inch pie; Use Basic Pie Crust
- 8 ounces Swiss or Jarlsberg cheese; cut into chunks
- 1 pound Ricotta cheese
- 3 Eggs
- 1 medium Onion; chopped fine
- 2 Cloves garlic; pressed
- ½ teaspoon White pepper
- 2 mediums Sized ripe tomatoes; peeled and thinly sliced
- 1 teaspoon Extra virgin olive oil
- 1 tablespoon Fresh snipped chives
- 1 tablespoon Chopped parsley
- 1 teaspoon Chopped fresh thyme;
- 1 teaspoon Chopped fresh basil;

INSTRUCTIONS:
a) Preheat oven to 450 degrees. Use a 9-inch by a 1-inch tart pan with removable bottom. Spray well with cooking spray or grease generously.
b) Press the pastry to fit into the pan. Trim smoothly about 1 inch beyond the edge of the pan, then fold back over the edge and crimp to make an attractive and sturdy fluted edge. Line the pan with aluminum foil that you have sprayed with cooking spray on both sides, then place an 8 or 9-inch glass pie pan inside the foil.
c) Turn the assembly upside down on the cookie sheet, and bake for 9 minutes. Remove pan from oven, turn over, and remove pie plate and foil.
d) Return to oven and bake 5 minutes longer. Remove from oven and set aside. Lower oven temperature to 350 degrees. In a blender or work bowl of a food processor, combine Jarlsberg, ricotta, eggs, onion, garlic, and pepper.
e) Whirl until smooth and well blended. Pour evenly into the baked shell, Place the pan on the cookie sheet. Bake for 25 to 30

minutes until the filling is partially set. Meanwhile, drain tomato slices on paper towels. Remove the tart from the oven.

f) Arrange tomato slices on top around the edge. Return to oven and bake for 30 to 35 minutes, until the knife inserted in the center comes out clean. Brush tomatoes with olive oil, and sprinkle with fresh herbs. Let stand 20 minutes. Remove tart pan sides by pressing upward on the removable bottom.

g) Place on a round platter, garnish with fresh herbs and serve.

81. Creamy garlic and cheese tart

Makes: 8 servings

INGREDIENTS:
- 1 Refrigerated pie crust
- 1 teaspoon flour
- 3 ounces cream cheese, Softened
- 6 ½ oz package garlic and spice Creamy spreadable cheese
- 2 tablespoons Butter
- 3 Eggs
- ¼ teaspoon Thyme
- ¼ teaspoon Ground red pepper
- ½ cup Milk or heavy cream

INSTRUCTIONS:
a) Preheat oven to 375F.
b) Line the pie dish with crust; dust lightly with flour.
c) Beat cheeses and butter until smooth. Add eggs, thyme, and red pepper; beat until light and creamy. Beat in milk just until blended. Pour into pie shell.
d) Bake, in the lower third of the oven, for about 30 minutes until light and puffy and a knife tests clean. If browning too quickly, cover it with foil during the last 10 minutes of cooking.
e) Place on a wire rack and cool to room temperature.

82. Curry and chutney cheese tart

Makes: 24 servings

INGREDIENTS:
- 16 ounces of Cream cheese
- 2 teaspoon Curry powder
- 2 tablespoon Sherry
- 8-ounce Cheddar cheese; shredded
- 4 Scallions; thinly sliced
- 9-ounce Jar of chutney

INSTRUCTIONS:
a) Place unwrapped packages of cream cheese in a 2-quart glass measure.
b) Microwave on medium for 2½ minutes.
c) Blend in curry powder and sherry. Fold in Cheddar and ¾ of onion; mix well.
d) Spoon the mixture onto a serving platter in an 8-inch circle.
e) Use a spatula to form a tart shape, building up sides while indenting the top.
f) Place chutney in blender and puree to a uniform mixture.
g) Pour in the indented area of the cheese tart. Chill until firm.
h) To serve, garnish the top with the remaining onion.

83. French cheese tart

Makes: 12 Servings

INGREDIENTS:
- 2 cups All-purpose flour; unsifted
- ¼ teaspoon Salt
- ½ teaspoon Baking powder
- ⅔ cup Butter or margarine
- ⅓ cup Granulated sugar
- 2 Egg yolks
- 2 tablespoons Heavy cream
- ½ teaspoon Grated lemon peel
- 4 tablespoons Butter or margarine
- ⅔ cup Granulated sugar
- 2 cups Dry cottage cheese
- 1 Egg yolk
- ¼ cup Heavy cream
- ⅓ cup Golden raisins
- ½ teaspoon Grated lemon rind
- 1 Egg white; slightly beaten
- Confectioner's sugar

INSTRUCTIONS:
a) Into a bowl, sift flour, salt, and baking powder.
b) With a pastry blender, cut in butter until the mixture resembles coarse crumbs.
c) Add ⅓ cup granulated sugar, 2 egg yolks, 2 tablespoons heavy cream, and ½ teaspoon lemon peel; with a fork, mix until pastry holds together.
d) Turn out on a lightly floured surface; knead until smooth, about 2 minutes.
e) Shape into a ball; wrap in waxed paper. Refrigerate the pastry for 30 minutes. Make Cheese
FILLING:

f) In a bowl with an electric mixer at High speed, beat butter, granulated sugar, and cottage cheese until well combined, about 3 minutes.

g) Add egg yolks and cream; beat well. Stir in raisins and lemon peel. Preheat oven to 350 F.

h) Lightly grease a 13x9x2" baking pan. Divide pastry in half.

i) On a lightly floured surface, roll out one half of the pastry into a 13x9" rectangle.

j) Fit into the bottom of the prepared pan. Pour into the filling, spreading evenly.

k) Divide the remaining pastry in half. Cut one half into 5 equal pieces.

l) On a board, roll each piece into a pencil-like strip 13" long.

m) Arrange these strips lengthwise, 1½ " apart on filling.

n) With the remaining pastry, make enough strips to fit diagonally, 1 ½ inches apart, across lengthwise strips.

o) Brush pastry strips with egg white.

p) Bake for 40 minutes or until golden brown. Let stand for 5 minutes.

q) Then sprinkle with confectioner's sugar, and cut into 3-inch squares. Serve warm.

84. Goat cheese and spinach tart

Makes: 8 servings

INGREDIENTS:
- ½ cup chopped onion
- 1 tablespoon olive oil
- 3 cups stemmed and washed spinach
- 5 eggs
- 1½ cups fresh goat cheese
- 2 cups heavy cream
- 1 salt; to taste
- 1 freshly-ground white pepper; to taste
- 1 nine-inch prebaked plain tart shell
- 2 tablespoon snipped chives
- 2 tablespoons finely-diced red bell pepper

INSTRUCTIONS:
a) Preheat oven to 350 degrees. In a skillet cook onion in oil until tender, 5 minutes; add spinach, a handful at a time, stirring.

b) Cook until spinach wilts, releases its liquid, and liquid evaporates.

c) Transfer to a bowl to cool. In another bowl beat eggs with goat cheese to blend thoroughly, add cream and stir in the cooled spinach mixture; season with salt and pepper. Fill tart shell. Bake for 30 minutes, until custard, is firmly set on the sides, but still slightly moist in the center.

d) Cool on a rack for about 10 minutes before cutting into wedges. Serve garnished with snipped chives and diced red pepper.

85. Golden pineapple-cheese tart

Makes: 12 Servings

INGREDIENTS:
- 2 cups Unsifted flour
- ¼ teaspoon Salt
- ½ teaspoon Baking powder
- ⅔ cup Butter or margarine
- ⅓ cup Sugar
- 2 Egg yolks
- 2 tablespoons Cream
- ½ teaspoon Grated lemon peel
- 8 ounces Crushed pineapple
- 4 tablespoons Butter or margarine
- ⅔ cup Sugar
- 16 ounces Cream cheese, softened
- 1 Egg yolk
- ¼ cup Heavy cream
- ½ cup Golden raisins
- 1 teaspoon Grated lemon peel

INSTRUCTIONS:
PASTRY:
a) In a bowl, sift flour, salt, and baking powder.
b) With a pastry blender, cut in ⅔ cup butter until the mixture resembles coarse crumbs.
c) Add sugar, 2 egg yolks, cream, and lemon peel.
d) Mix with hands just until the mixture holds together. Flour and knead for about 2 minutes,
e) Refrigerate pastry on waxed paper for 30 minutes.
f) Drain pineapple, and preheat oven to 350 degrees F. Grease 10-inch spring form pan.
g) Remove the side of the pan.
FILLING:
h) In a bowl, beat butter, sugar, and cream cheese at high speed until blended.

i) Add egg yolk and cream. Stir in pineapple, raisins, and lemon peel. Set aside.
j) Place ¾ of the pastry dough into the bottom of the spring form pan.
k) Roll out the dough to fit the pan. Bake 12 minutes or until golden; cool. Replace the side of the spring from the pan.
l) Pour filling into the pan - spreading evenly.
m) Decorate the top of the filling with the remaining pastry.
n) Bake for 40 minutes or until golden brown. Cool for 10 minutes. Sprinkle with confectioner's sugar. Serve warm or at room temperature. Store refrigerated.

86. Grape and currant tart with fontina cheese

Makes: 8 servings

INGREDIENTS:
- ½ cup Boiling water
- ¼ cup Dried currants
- 6 slices White bread ¾ ounce each slice
- Vegetable cooking spray
- 1½ cup Skim milk; divided
- 1¼ cup Diced fontina cheese 5 ounces
- 1¼ cup Seedless red grapes; halved
- 2 tablespoons All-purpose flour
- ⅓ cup Sugar
- 2 tablespoons Yellow cornmeal
- 1 teaspoon Grated lemon rind
- 3 Egg whites; lightly beaten
- 1 Egg; lightly beaten
- 1 teaspoon Extra-virgin olive oil
- 1 tablespoon Sugar
- 2 teaspoons Chopped fresh rosemary

INSTRUCTIONS:
a) Preheat oven to 350 degrees.
b) Combine boiling water and currants; let stand for 15 minutes. Drain and set aside. Trim crusts from bread; discard crusts.
c) Cut each slice into 4 triangles; place triangles in a single layer in a 10-inch quiche dish coated with cooking spray. Pour ½ cup milk over the bread; let stand for 5 minutes. Top with currants, cheese, and grapes.
d) Place flour in a bowl, and gradually add the remaining 1 cup of milk, stirring with a wire whisk until blended.
e) Stir in ⅓ cup sugar, cornmeal, lemon rind, egg whites, and egg; pour over the tart. Drizzle oil over tart, and sprinkle with 1 tablespoon of sugar and rosemary.
f) Bake for 45 minutes or until set; let cool on a wire rack

87. Herbed cheese tarts

Makes: 24 servings

INGREDIENTS:
- ⅓ cup Fine dry bread crumbs or finely crushed zwieback
- 8 ounces Package of cream cheese, softened
- ¾ cup Cream-style cottage cheese
- ½ cup Shredded Swiss cheese
- 1 tablespoon All-purpose flour
- ¼ teaspoon Dried basil, crushed
- ⅛ teaspoon Garlic powder
- 2 Eggs
- nonstick spray coating
- dairy sour cream
- sliced or slivered pitted ripe olives, red caviar
- roasted red pepper

INSTRUCTIONS:
a) For the crust, spray twenty-four 1¾-inch muffin cups with nonstick spray coating.
b) Sprinkle bread crumbs or crushed zwieback onto the bottom and sides to coat.
c) Shake pans to remove excess crumbs. Set aside.
d) In a small mixer bowl, combine cream cheese, cottage cheese, Swiss cheese, flour, basil, and garlic powder. Beat with an electric mixer on medium speed just till fluffy.
e) Add eggs; beat on low speed just till combined. Do not overbeat.
f) Fill each crumb-lined muffin cup with 1 tablespoon of the cheese mixture. Bake in a 375-degree F oven for 15 minutes or till centers appear set.
g) Cool in pans on wire racks for 10 minutes. Remove from pans.
h) Cool thoroughly on wire racks.
i) To serve, spread tops with sour cream. Garnish with olives, caviar, chives, and/or red pepper and olive cut-outs. Makes: 24 tarts.

j) Bake and cool tarts as directed, except do not spread with sour cream or top with garnish.
k) Cover and chill in the refrigerator for up to 48 hours. Let tarts stand at room temperature for 30 minutes before serving.
l) Spread with sour cream and garnish as directed.

88. Mediterranean cheese tart

Makes: 12 Servings

INGREDIENTS:
- 8 Sheets frozen phyllo dough; thawed
- ¼ cup Butter; melted
- ¼ cup Parmesan cheese; grated
- ½ cup Onion; chopped
- 1 teaspoon Fresh rosemary; snipped
- ¼ teaspoon Dried rosemary, crushed)
- 1 tablespoon Olive oil
- 5 ounces Frozen chopped spinach; thawed
- ⅓ cup Toasted pine nuts or walnuts
- 1 Egg
- 1 cup Ricotta cheese
- ½ cup Feta cheese; crumbled
- ¼ cup Oil pack sundried tomatoes; drained
- ¼ teaspoon Coarsely ground pepper
- 1 tablespoon Parmesan cheese; grated

INSTRUCTIONS:
a) Unfold phyllo; cover it with plastic wrap or a damp towel to keep it from drying out.
b) On a dry working surface, place one sheet of phyllo; brush with butter.
c) Top with another sheet of phyllo, brush with butter, and sprinkle with 1 tablespoon of Parmesan cheese.
d) Repeat with remaining phyllo sheets, butter, and Parmesan.
e) Using kitchen shears, trim the phyllo into an 11" circle.
f) Ease the phyllo evenly into the prepared pan, pleating as necessary and being careful not to tear the phyllo. Cover the pan with a damp towel; set aside.
g) For the filling: cook onions and rosemary in olive oil in a medium saucepan until onions are tender. Stir in spinach and pine nuts.
h) Spread in the phyllo-lined spring form pan. Set aside.

i) Lightly beat egg in a bowl. Stir in ricotta, feta, tomatoes, and pepper. Carefully spread over the spinach mixture. Sprinkle with 1 tablespoon of Parmesan cheese.

j) Place the spring form pan on a shallow baking pan on the oven rack. Bake in a 350 oven for 35 to 40 minutes or until the center appears nearly set when shaken.

k) Cool tart in spring form pan on a wire rack for 5 minutes. Loosen the sides of the pan. Cool for 15 to 30 minutes more. Before serving, remove the sides of the spring from the pan. Serve warm.

89. Lemon-cheese tarts

Makes: 1 serving

INGREDIENTS:
- ¼ cup Lemon juice
- Grated rind of 1 ½ lemons
- ½ cup Plus 1 tablespoon of sugar
- 2 Eggs; beaten
- ¼ cup Butter or margarine -Cream Cheese Shells---
- ½ cup Butter or margarine; softened
- 3 ounces Package of cream cheese; softened
- 1 cup All-purpose flour
- Whipped cream

INSTRUCTIONS:
a) Combine lemon juice, rind, and sugar on top of a double boiler; stir in eggs and butter.
b) Cook over boiling water, stirring constantly until thickened.
c) Spoon filling into Cream Cheese Shells; garnish with whipped cream.
d) Combine butter and cream cheese, mixing until smooth; add flour, mixing well. Chill for 1 hour.
e) Shape dough into 1-inch balls; place each in a well-greased miniature muffin cup, shaping into a shell.
f) Bake at 350 degrees for 25 minutes. Allow cooling before filling.

90. Papaya-cream cheese tart with macadamia nuts

Makes: 8 servings

INGREDIENTS:
- 2 cups Flour
- 6 ounces of cold unsalted butter cubes
- ¼ teaspoon Salt
- ½ teaspoon Sugar
- ⅓ cup Cold water
- 12 ounces Cream cheese
- 4 ounces Heavy whipping cream
- ½ cup Powdered sugar
- ½ teaspoon Vanilla extract
- 1 Very ripe papaya, peeled, Cut into ¼" slices
- ½ cup Peach glaze, melted
- ½ cup Macadamia nuts, toasted
- 8 ounces of Bitter chocolate
- 8 ounces of Semisweet chocolate
- 2½ cups Heavy cream
- 4 tablespoons Warm water

INSTRUCTIONS:
a) Prepare the Tart Shell-- Sift together the flour, salt, and sugar. Coat butter cubes with the flour mixture and water and knead until malleable, but not homogeneous.
b) Leave bits of plain butter, otherwise, the dough becomes too elastic. Gently roll dough to the ¼-inch thickness and lay it onto a tart pan. Trim the edges and poke the bottom of the pastry with a fork. Bake in the oven at 350 degrees F for about ten minutes or until the tart shell browns slightly. Chill.
c) Prepare Cream Cheese Filling-- Whip whipping cream until it forms soft peaks. In a mixer, beat cream cheese until it becomes fluffy. Fold in whipped cream, powdered sugar, and vanilla extract.
d) Set aside.
e) Fill the tart shell with cream cheese mixture.

f) Arrange papaya slices in a pinwheel design over the top of the cream cheese. Place macadamia nuts in the center of the tart. With a pastry brush, coat the top of the tart with peach glaze. Refrigerate for ½ hour before serving.

g) Prepare Chocolate Sauce-- Heat bitter chocolate, semisweet chocolate, heavy cream, and warm water in a saucepan, stirring frequently, until the sauce is a smooth consistency.

h) To Serve-- Slice tart into 8 pieces. Drizzle chocolate sauce onto a plate and place one piece of the tart on each plate.

91. Ricotta cheese and spinach tart

Makes: 6 Servings

INGREDIENTS:
- 14oz Strong Plain Flour
- 1 pinch Salt
- 1 pack Waitrose Fresh Basil and Thyme, chopped
- 3 tablespoons olive oil
- 3 Eggs, beaten
- 250g tub Ricotta Cheese
- 500g pack of frozen whole-leaf spinach
- Freshly grated nutmeg
- 2 Eggs
- 1 ¾ ounces Pine kernels, toasted
- 1 Lemon; zest of
- 3 ½ ounces Grated Parmesan
- Salt and freshly ground black pepper
- Milk to glaze

INSTRUCTIONS:
a) Sift the flour into a bowl and add the salt and herbs.
b) Make a well in the center. Add the oil and then gradually add the eggs.
c) Mix until smooth, adding a little water if required.
d) Knead for 10 minutes, then wrap in cling film and place in a refrigerator for 30 minutes.
e) Combine all the filling ingredients.
f) On a floured surface, roll out two-thirds of the pasta and use it to line a square tin.
g) Spoon the filling into the pasta and smooth it out to cover the base.
h) Roll out the remaining pasta and cover the top.
i) Wet and seal the edges with a little water.
j) Trim off any excess pasta and brush with a little milk, prick, and place in the center of a preheated oven.
k) Bake at 400ºF for 25-30 minutes until golden on top.

92. Southwest cheese tart

Makes: 8 servings

INGREDIENTS:
- 1 tablespoon oil
- ½ cup chopped red bell pepper
- ½ cup chopped onion
- 1 tablespoon minced garlic
- 1 tablespoon minced jalapeno pepper
- 4 eggs
- 2 cups heavy cream
- 2 cups jalapeno jack cheese
- 1 cup roasted corn kernels; plus
- 1 extra roasted corn kernel; for garnish
- 1 cup cooked black beans; rinsed
- ½ teaspoon ground cumin
- ¼ teaspoon chili powder
- 1 salt; to taste
- 1 freshly-ground white pepper; to taste
- 1 nine-inch pre-baked tart shell
- 1 serving pico de gallo
- 1 chopped cilantro; for garnish

INSTRUCTIONS:
a) In a skillet heat oil and cook bell pepper, onion, and garlic until tender; set aside to cool.
b) In a bowl whisk eggs and cream until combined; stir in sautéed vegetables and remaining ingredients, and season with spices, salt, and pepper. Pour egg mixture into the tart shell and bake for 30 minutes or until custard is firm to the touch.
c) Cool briefly before cutting. Serve with Pico De Gallo alongside, sprinkled with roasted corn kernels and chopped cilantro.

MUSHROOM TART

93. Exotic mushroom tart

Makes: 8 servings

INGREDIENTS:
- 2½ cup Flour; plus
- 2 tablespoons Flour
- 2 teaspoons Salt
- ½ teaspoon Cayenne
- 1 cup Lard
- 2 tablespoons Ice water
- 2 tablespoons Butter
- ½ cup Minced onions
- Salt; to taste
- Freshly-ground black pepper; to taste
- 4 cups Sliced exotic mushrooms
- 2 teaspoons Chopped garlic
- 2 cups Heavy cream
- 3 Eggs
- 1 dash of Hot pepper sauce
- 1 dash Worcestershire sauce
- 1 cup Grated white cheddar cheese
- 4 ounces Parmigiano-Reggiano cheese; shaved
- 2 cups Pea shoots

INSTRUCTIONS:
a) Drizzle of white truffle oil
b) In a bowl, combine 2½ cups of flour, 2 teaspoons of salt, and ¼ teaspoon of cayenne. Cut in the lard with a pastry blender until the mixture resembles a coarse meal.
c) Add the ice water and mix until the dough comes away from the sides of the bowl. Form the dough into a ball and cover it with plastic wrap. Place in the refrigerator and chill for 1 hour.
d) Preheat the oven to 350 degrees. Remove the dough from the refrigerator and let sit for about 5 minutes. Lightly dust a work surface with the remaining flour. Roll the dough out into a 12-inch round about ¼-inch thick.

e) Fold the dough into fourths and place it in a 10-inch tart pan. Roll a wooden rolling pin over the pan to cut off the excess dough.

f) Prick the bottom of the crust all over with a fork. In a medium sauté pan, over medium heat, melt the butter. Add the onions. Season with salt and pepper. Sauté for 1 minute. Add the mushrooms. Season with salt and pepper.

g) Continue to sauté for 3 to 4 minutes or until the mushrooms are wilted.

h) Stir in the garlic and remove from the heat. Cool completely. In a bowl, whisk the cream and eggs together. Season with ¾ of a teaspoon of salt, pepper, hot pepper sauce, and Worcestershire sauce.

i) Mix well. Pour the mushroom mixture into the pastry shell. Sprinkle the cheese over the mushrooms. Pour the cream mixture over the cheese.

j) Bake until the center sets and the top is golden, about 55 minutes. Remove from the oven and let cool for 5 minutes before slicing to serve. In a bowl, toss the pea shoots with the truffle oil. Season with salt and pepper. To serve, place a slice of the tart in the center of each plate.

k) Garnish each with a pile of pea shoots.

94. Flaky mushroom tarts

Makes: 30 Servings

INGREDIENTS:
- 1 pound Fresh Mushrooms
- 1 medium Onion
- ½ cup Parsley; fresh
- ½ cup White wine
- dash Hot pepper sauce
- 4 Phyllo dough; thawed
- 6 tablespoons Butter, melted
- 4 ounces Monterey jack cheese; cubed

INSTRUCTIONS:
a) Preheat oven to 400.
b) Chop mushrooms, onion, and parsley. In a large skillet, combine mushrooms, onion, parsley, wine, and hot pepper sauce. Cover.
c) Cook for 5 - 7 minutes until mushrooms are tender, stirring occasionally.
d) Uncover and cook until the liquid has evaporated. Cool.
e) Lightly brush 1 sheet of phyllo dough with melted butter.
f) Place another sheet of dough on top of the first sheet.
g) Brush with butter. Repeat with the remaining dough and butter.
h) Cut the stack into 2 - ½ inch squares.
i) Gently press each piece into an ungreased mini muffin pan.
j) Place about 2 teaspoons of mushroom mixture in each cup. Top each with a cheese cube.
k) Bake for 15 - 18 minutes or until light brown. Serve warm.

95. Grilled eggplant and mushroom tart

Makes: 8 servings

INGREDIENTS:
- Cooking Spray
- 1 large Eggplant; peeled and sliced in ½" slices
- 6 large Potatoes; peeled and sliced in ½" slices
- 6 large Portabella mushrooms; caps and stems separated, caps left whole, stems sliced
- Olive oil for brushing
- 1 tablespoon Olive oil; for bread crumbs
- Salt and Pepper
- ¼ cup Parsley; chopped
- ¼ cup Basil; julienne
- ¾ cup Grated Fresh Parmesan cheese; or Pecorino Romano
- 1 cup Fresh bread crumbs
- 1 tablespoon Olive oil
- 1 small Onion; minced
- 1 Celery stalk; minced
- 4 large Tomatoes; seeded and coarsely chopped
- ½ cup Grated carrots
- 1 teaspoon Fresh thyme; or ½ teaspoon dried thyme
- 1 teaspoon Fresh lemon juice
- 2 teaspoons Fresh parsley; chopped

INSTRUCTIONS:
a) Make Relish: Heat the oil in a nonreactive saucepan. Stir in the onion and celery and sauté over medium heat for 3 minutes.

b) Stir in the tomatoes, carrots, thyme, and salt and pepper to taste. Simmer the relish gently until most of the liquid has cooked off. Remove from the heat.

c) Right before serving, rewarm the relish. Remove from the heat and stir in the lemon juice and parsley.

d) Spray the grill rack well with cooking spray. Preheat the grill to medium-high heat. Brush eggplant, potatoes, and mushrooms well with olive oil and season on both sides with salt and pepper.

e) Spray a 9" cake pan or tart pan well with cooking spray. Heat the pan either in the oven or on top of your grill, if large enough. Keep hot.

f) Grill all vegetables on both sides until well browned and softened. Slice mushroom caps into thin slices. Make layers in the pie or tart pan - eggplant, potato, mushroom, sprinkling some of the parsley, basil, and grated cheese in between each vegetable layer. Keep hot.

g) In a small skillet, heat the 3 tablespoons of olive oil on medium-high heat until hot. Add bread crumbs and sauté until golden brown.

h) Top tart with bread crumbs. Serve immediately with a small pool of tomato relish under each wedge.

96. Mushroom phyllo tarts

Makes: 4 servings

INGREDIENTS:
- ¾ cup Dairy sour cream
- 3 ounces cream cheese; softened
- ¼ cup Dry bread crumbs
- 1 tablespoon Dried dill weed
- ½ teaspoon Salt
- 1 tablespoon Lemon juice
- 4.5 Oz Green Giant sliced mushrooms
- 1 Garlic clove; minced
- ½ cup Butter or margarine
- 8 Frozen phyllo pastry sheets

INSTRUCTIONS:
a) Heat oven to 350 degrees.
b) In a bowl, combine sour cream, cream cheese, bread crumbs, dill weed, salt, and lemon juice; blend well. Stir in sliced mushrooms. Set aside.
c) To make garlic butter, in a small skillet over low heat, cook garlic in butter until tender, stirring constantly. Coat 16 muffin cups with garlic butter. Set aside.
d) Brush a large cookie sheet with garlic butter. Unroll phyllo sheets; cover with plastic wrap or a towel. Brush one phyllo sheet lightly with garlic butter; place on the buttered cookie sheet.
e) Brush the second phyllo sheet lightly with garlic butter; place it on top of the first buttered sheet. Repeat with remaining phyllo sheets. With a sharp knife, cut through all layers of phyllo sheets to make 16 rectangles.
f) Lightly press each rectangle into a garlic-buttered muffin cup. Spoon a heaping tablespoonful of sour cream mixture into each cup. Top each with the whole mushroom, pushing the stem into the filling. Drizzle with remaining garlic butter.
g) Bake at 350 degrees for 18-20 minutes or until light golden brown.

97. Smoky mushroom tart

Makes: 8 servings

INGREDIENTS:
- ⅓ BUTTER PASTRY dough
- 1 Egg white, lightly beaten
- 2 tablespoons Butter
- 10 ounces Fresh mushrooms, sliced
- 7 ounces Shitake mushrooms, stems discarded
- And mushrooms sliced
- 1 tablespoon Minced fresh garlic
- 2 teaspoons Dried oregano, crushed
- ⅛ teaspoon Ground black pepper
- ½ pounds Smoked mozzarella cheese, thinly sliced
- 2 tablespoons Grates asiago or Parmesan cheese
- ⅓ cup Walnut pieces
- 1 tablespoon Chopped flat-leaf parsley

INSTRUCTIONS:
a) Preheat oven to 400 F. On a lightly floured surface roll the dough to a 14-inch round.
b) Transfer to an 11-inch tart pan with removable bottom.
c) Trim edges; prick the bottom with the tines of a fork.
d) Line the pastry shell with foil and pastry weights, dried beans, or raw rice. Bake for 15 minutes.
e) Remove foil and weights.
f) Bake 5 to 6 minutes longer or just until the pastry starts to turn golden. Brush with egg white; bake 1 minute longer.
g) Cool completely on a wire rack. In a large skillet, melt butter over medium-low heat.
h) Add mushrooms, garlic, oregano, and pepper.
i) Sauté until mushrooms are golden and liquid has evaporated, about 8 minutes; cool to room temperature.
j) Cover the bottom of the tart shell with mozzarella, cutting slices to fill in spaces.

k) Top with the mushroom mixture then sprinkles with asiago and walnuts.

l) Bake for 20 minutes. Cool for 5 minutes on the wire rack before removing the outer ring. Serve warm.

98. Triple mushroom tart

Makes: 10 servings

INGREDIENTS:
- 1 Unbaked refrigerated pie Crust
- 1 cup Chopped fresh shiitake Mushrooms
- 1 cup Sliced fresh white or brown Mushrooms
- 1 cup Chopped fresh Oyster Mushrooms
- ¼ teaspoon Dried marjoram
- 2 tablespoons Butter
- ¾ cup Shredded Gruyere cheese
- ¾ cup Shredded Swiss cheese
- ½ cup Chopped Canadian bacon
- 2 Eggs, slightly beaten
- ½ cup Milk
- 1 tablespoon Snipped fresh chives
- Canadian bacon, cut in thin
- Wedges, optional

INSTRUCTIONS:

a) Press pastry into a 9" tart pan with removable bottom. Flute; trim evenly with top. Line with a double layer of foil; bake at 450F. 8 minutes.

b) Remove foil, and continue baking for 4-5- minutes until set and dry.

c) Turn oven to 375F.

d) Cook mushrooms until tender in butter, 4-5 minutes, until the liquid is evaporated.

e) Remove from heat.

f) Blend Gruyere, Swiss cheeses, and Canadian bacon.

g) Add mushrooms, milk, eggs, and chives. Pour into tart crust.

h) Bake for about 20 minutes until set and golden.

i) Cool in a pan on a wire rack for 10-15 minutes. Remove.

j) Cut into wedges and garnish with Canadian bacon wedges.

99. Wild mushroom and goat's cheese tart

Makes: 2 servings

INGREDIENTS:
- 375-gram ready-rolled puff pastry
- 1 Egg; beaten
- 50 grams Butter
- 250 grams Mixed mushrooms
- 2 large Clove garlic
- 1 small Bunch of flat-leaf parsley
- 1 tablespoon Balsamic vinegar
- 150 grams of Creamed goat's cheese
- 2 tablespoons Olive oil
- 100 grams Cherry tomatoes
- 1 Lemon
- 1 small Bunch of basil
- 100 grams of Baby spinach leaves

INSTRUCTIONS:
a) Preheat oven to 220c/425f/Gas 7.
b) Place the pastry on a lightly floured surface, cut out two 12x15cm/5"x6" rectangles, and put them onto a non-stick baking sheet.
c) Brush over the beaten egg and, using the point of a sharp knife, mark a 1cm/14" border inside each tart.
d) Prick the center rectangle all over with a fork and bake in the oven for eight minutes until well-risen and golden.
e) Heat a large frying pan with butter. Roughly cut the mushrooms into bite-sized pieces. Finely slice the garlic and add with the mushrooms. Fry for 3-4 minutes until cooked and golden.
f) Roughly chop the parsley, add half with the balsamic vinegar, and cook for a minute. Season with salt and pepper, and reserve. Place the goat's cheese in a bowl, add the remaining parsley, and mix well. Season with pepper.

g) Remove the pastry from the oven. Carefully cut around the inner rectangle of the pastry and, using a fish slice, flatten the centerpiece of the pastry.

h) Return the pastry case to the oven for another 4-5 minutes until cooked through and golden.

i) For the Salad: Warm the olive oil in a small pan. Cut the cherry tomatoes in half and add to the pan with the lemon zest and a squeeze of juice. Mix well and season with salt and pepper.

j) Put the spinach into a bowl and pour over the warm dressing.

k) Remove the tarts from the oven, spoon in the goat's cheese, and top with the warm mushrooms. Transfer to a plate and serve with the salad.

100. Wild mushroom and pecorino tart

Makes: 1 serving

INGREDIENTS:
- 3 tablespoons Olive oil
- 2 Handfuls mixed wild mushrooms
- 1 large Clovee garlic; finely chopped
- ¼ Lemon; zest of
- 2 tablespoons Flat parsley; coarsely chopped
- 2 Sheets of puff pastry
- The thickness of 2 matchsticks
- 75 grams Young pecorino cheese; thinly sliced

INSTRUCTIONS:
a) Preheat the oven to 200C.
b) Heat the olive oil in a frying pan, add the mushrooms, season, and sauté, briskly until cooked.
c) Stir in the garlic, lemon zest, and parsley. Remove from the heat and set aside.
d) Oil a baking sheet. Place two sheets of pastry on it. Place the mushrooms in a layer in the middle of each sheet. Transfer to the oven and cook for 20-25 minutes, or until golden brown.
e) Remove from the oven and top with Pecorino and return to the oven for 3-4 minutes. Remove and serve immediately.

CONCLUSION

Enjoying some store-bought tarts is one of life's simple pleasures, but the thought of trying to bake a tart yourself might seem like a daunting task, especially if you've only tried making cookies and brownies. If you are looking to try making tarts but don't know where to start, this COOKBOOK will bring you through the types of tarts, and recipes you'll need to get started. Enjoy!

Ingram Content Group UK Ltd.
Milton Keynes UK
UKHW020623210623
423802UK00010B/129